ABOUT THE AUTHOF

Barbara Cartland, the world's most famous romantic novelist, who is also an historian, playwright, lecturer, political speaker and television personality, has now written over 350 books and sold over 350 million books all over the world.

She has also had many historical works published and has written four autobiographies as well as the biographies of her mother and that of her brother, Ronald Cartland, who was the first Member of Parliament to be killed in the last war. This book has a preface by Sir Winston Churchill and has just been republished with an introduction by Sir Arthur Bryant.

Love at the Helm, a novel written with the help and inspiration of the late Earl Mountbatten of Burma, uncle of His Royal Highness Prince Philip, is being sold for the Mountbatten Memorial Trust.

Miss Cartland in 1978 sang an Album of love songs with the Royal Philharmonic Orchestra.

In 1976, by writing twenty-one books, she broke the world record for the number of published works by one author in a year. In subsequent years, however, she broke her own record repeatedly with twenty-four, twenty, twenty-three, twenty-four and twenty-four. In the *Guinness Book of Records* she is listed as the world's top-selling author.

In private life Barbara Cartland, who is a Dame of the Order of St. John of Jerusalem, Chairman of the St. John Council in Hertfordshire and Deputy President of the St. John Ambulance Brigade, has fought for better conditions and salaries for midwives and nurses.

She has championed the cause for old people, had the law altered regarding Gypsies and founded the first Romany Gypsy camp in the world.

Barbara Cartland is deeply interested in Vitamin Therapy, and is President of the National Association for Health.

Her designs 'Decorating with Love' are being sold all over the U.S.A. and the National Home Fashions League made her, in 1981, 'Woman of Achievement'.

OTHER BOOKS BY BARBARA CARTLAND

Romantic novels – over 300, the most recently published being:

The Call of the Highlands
Love and the Marquis
Kneel for Mercy
Riding to the Moon
Wish for Love
Mission to Monte Carlo
A Miracle in Music
A Marriage Made in Heaven
Light from the Gods
From Hate to Love
Love on the Wind
The Duke Comes Home
Journey to a Star
Love and Linda
The Unwanted Wedding
Gypsy Magic
Help from the Heart
A Duke in Danger
Lights, Laughter and a Lady
The Unbreakable Spell

The Dream and the Glory
(in aid of the St. John Ambulance Brigade)

Autobiographical and Biographical

The Isthmus Years 1919–1939
The Years of Opportunity 1939–1945
I Search for Rainbows 1945–1976
We Danced All Night 1919–1929
Ronald Cartland (with a Foreword by Sir Winston Churchill)
Polly My Wonderful Mother
I Seek the Miraculous

Historical

Bewitching Women
The Outrageous Queen (the story of Queen Christina of Sweden)
The Scandalous Life of King Carol
The Private Life of Elizabeth, Empress of Austria
Josephine, Empress of France
Diane de Poitiers
Metternich – the Passionate Diplomat

Sociology

You in the Home
The Fascinating Forties
Marriage for Moderns
Be Vivid, Be Vital
Love, Life and Sex
Vitamins for Vitality
Husbands and Wives
Men Are Wonderful
Etiquette
The Many Facets of Love
Sex and the Teenager
The Book of Charm
Living Together
The Youth Secret
The Magic of Honey
Book of Beauty and Health

Keep Young and Beautiful by Barbara Cartland and Elinor Glyn

Cookery

Barbara Cartland's Health Food Cookery Book
Food for Love
Magic of Honey Cookbook
Recipes for Lovers

Editor of

The Common Problems by Ronald Cartland (with a preface by the Rt. Hon. the Earl of Selborne, P.C.)
Barbara Cartland's Library of Love
Barbara Cartland's Library of Ancient Wisdom
Written with Love (passionate love letters)

Drama

Blood Money
French Dressing

Philosophy

Touch the Stars

Radio Operetta

The Rose and the Violet (music by Mark Lubbock). Performed in 1942

Radio Plays

The Caged Bird: An Episode in the Life of Elizabeth Empress of Austria. Performed in 1957

General

Barbara Cartland's Book of Useless Information, with a Foreword by The Earl Mountbatten of Burma (in aid of the United Colleges)
Love and Lovers (Picture Book)
The Light of Love (Prayer Book)
Barbara Cartland's Scrapbook (in aid of the Royal Photographic Museum)
Romantic Royal Marriages
Barbara Cartland's Book of Celebrities

Verse

Lines of Life and Love

Music

An Album of Love Songs sung with the Royal Philharmonic Orchestra

Film

The Flame is Love

Cartoons

Barbara Cartland Romances (Book of Cartoons) has recently been published and seventy-five newspapers in the U.S.A. and other parts of the world carry her strip cartoons

Barbara Cartland's Book of Celebrities

QUARTET BOOKS
LONDON MELBOURNE NEW YORK

First published by Quartet Books Limited 1982

Quartet Books Limited
A member of the Namara Group
27/29 Goodge Street, London W1P 1FD

Copyright © Barbara Cartland, 1982

British Library Cataloguing in Publication Data

Cartland, Barbara
Barbara Cartland's book of celebrities.
1. Biography–20th century
I. Title
920'.009'047 CT106

ISBN 0-7043-3395-3

Typeset by MC Typeset, Rochester, Kent
Printed and bound in Great Britain by Mackays of Chatham Limited, Kent

Contents

AUTHOR'S NOTE

It was Lord Northcliffe in the early Twenties who realised that, in addition to news, people liked to read about personalities.

"Get more names in the papers," he instructed his editors, "and the more aristocrats, the better!"

Later the Editor of the *Daily Mirror* ordered his reporters to – "find out what makes them tick. Dig deep, and make it dirty."

It was all part of mankind's eternal search to discover himself. The difficulty having been accentuated by modern thinking, which has produced the phony ideal of 'equality'.

This is completely impossible when by the miracle of creation out of the billions and billions of bodies born not one is exactly like another.

Also the mind, personality and character of each individual are a mixture of hereditary tendencies, the influence of environment and, more complicated still, the development of other 'lives'.

One cannot discredit the last without explaining how Mozart could play the violin perfectly at four, and Victoria Taylor, aged three, is an acknowledged expert at chess.

What I have found in a long life of meeting many and varied people is that their success or failure rests on their personal transmission of the life force.

Life cannot die – that is a contradiction in terms – only the body wears out and is discarded, while the life force used by that particular individual goes back to its source.

How much we imprint ourselves on the life force we have used during the years it has flowed through us is decided by us personally. But the strength and power of it determine our influence and impact in the world in which we live.

I have seen and felt this life force emanating from many famous and celebrated people for good or bad, in a greater or lesser degree, according to their capability to draw on it.

The people I have included in this book all had drive, determination and that vulgar, but very expressive word 'guts'. They were also sensitive, vulnerable when one least expected it, shy, apprehensive and sometimes afraid.

And yet they had an aura which was inescapable. One felt it as soon as they entered a room because they made the tempo rise, and one either loved or hated them.

Often expressive, invariably controversial, eccentric but exciting, they are indivisibly all part of the history of this turbulent, changing, traumatic century.

Just as the Chinese tried to depict in their paintings the world behind the world, I sometimes had a glimpse of what lay behind the public image. It intrigued and thrilled me, or made me feel compassionate and protective.

The stories I relate may seem trivial, insignificant and of no importance, but to me they were significant, touching and very human.

Barbara Cartland

There are those
Through whom the stream flows slowly,
Often dim and grey, but never still.
Its flow unceasing, ceaseless,
Till – as the dawn breaks in a sable sky –
The purpose of its moving stands revealed,
The path of God – the leaping flame of life!

MICHAEL ARLEN

Michael Arlen – Dikrān Kuyumjian – introduced as "the only Armenian who hasn't been massacred", was the High Priest of the Twenties.

Actually he had never been to Armenia as his parents were Bulgarians who escaped from the first Turkish massacres and settled in Manchester.

After trying to become a doctor at Edinburgh University, Michael came to London to be a journalist. He knew nobody and lived alone in a small room over a shop in Shepherd's Market.

He was short, dark, exotically debonair, imaginative, wildly ambitious and, more than anything else, witty.

Remarks like "he was every other inch a gentleman" came naturally to him. He put into words the gaiety, the recklessness, the chivalry, the courage and bitter-sweet flavour of the Twenties.

He showed us ourselves not only as we were but as we wanted to be, and could anything have been more intriguing?

We were *These Charming People*, *Young Men in Love*, the love-torn desperate characters in *The Green Hat*.

Yet underneath the froth, the romance and the irresistible allure of Michael's books, there was something deeper – a desire to hurt, to burst the bubbles we blew so bravely.

He was a success overnight, with reprints, plays and films!

Rich and famous, knowing 'everybody', generous with his money, he was still acutely aware of being a stranger, a foreigner.

One evening I went with a young man to dine with his cousin, the most beautiful of all the beautiful, blue-blooded leaders of Mayfair Society.

She was unhappy with her husband and Michael the fourth guest was obviously there as a consolation.

Immaculately, if slightly flamboyantly, dressed, he courted her with a brilliant seduction of words, glances and impeccable good manners which would have been acclaimed on any stage.

That I realised was what it was, a skilful performance, and underneath there was still tension, insecurity and perhaps aggression.

When dinner ended the 'Beauty' said:

"I'm going to show Michael the house!"

As they left the room he looked back and there was in his eyes an

Michael and his beautiful Greek wife with their son. He also had a yellow Rolls-Royce, and his real name was Dikrān Kuyumjian.

Successful but not so seductive.

expression of triumph and at the same time, a mocking cynicism which was unmistakable.

It was as if he said in the words of Aly Khan, the outstanding Casanova of the Thirties:

"They called me a bloody nigger and I paid them out by winning all their women!"

In the next few years Michael went from success to success, with invitations to every party, a table reserved at the exclusive Embassy Club, and a yellow Rolls-Royce.

He married a beautiful Greek Countess, had a home in Hollywood, a villa at Cannes and a speedboat.

A long time later I saw Michael in London, and I asked rather tactlessly: "Why aren't you writing?"

Actually I knew the answer, the glittering dancing world of the Twenties had faded into the apprehension and depression of the threadbare Thirties. Michael's books were no longer sensational, no longer true to life. The Bright Young People had grown staid and serious.

He did not answer for a moment. Then he said:

"I've forgotten how to hate."

KING LOUIS

In 1924 Louis's *legato* trumpet style is new to New York and he is 'scat' singing in *Everybody Loves My Baby*.

LOUIS ARMSTRONG

In 1933 I said to a young man who was taking me out one evening:

"I would like to go to the Palladium to hear this man they call 'the coloured phenomenon'. His name is Louis Armstrong."

"I'll take you," was the reply, "but you won't like him. I hear lots of people walked out!"

I insisted on going because I was interested in jazz which had followed ragtime, although few people in England knew much about it.

I thought Louis Armstrong fantastic! His top notes seemed to touch my heart, as they still do.

I noticed a few men sneaking out of the stalls, and there were a number of empty seats after the interval, but the majority of listeners were entranced.

Louis' first number was *Them There Eyes*, his second *When You're Smiling*, and his third one which was very much a part of my life in the Twenties *Chinatown, My Chinatown*.

One of the newspapers wrote:

> Top F's bubble about all over the place, and never once does he miss one. He is enormously fond of the lip-trill, which he accomplishes by shaking the instrument wildly with his right hand. He works with a microphone and loud speakers – except for his trumpet-playing which varies from a veritable whisper to roof-raising strength, mostly the latter.

After praising Armstrong's showmanship and good humour, the writer concluded:

> All the time he is singing he carries a handkerchief in his hand and mops his face – perspiration positively drops off him. He puts enough energy into his half-hour's performance to last the average man several years. He is, in short, a unique phenomenon, an electric personality – easily the greatest America has sent us so far.

A batch of twenty (or was it forty?) freshly laundered white handkerchiefs was on hand for each performance, and Louis made lavish use of them.

In the years to come he was to make jazz an international language and he also made it a way of life.

Most early jazzmen put on an act, but he was a natural performer.

"You don't pose, never, that's the last thing you do," he said once, "because the minute you pose you're through as a jazzman. Jazz is only what you are."

I did not hear Louis Armstrong in person again until December 1956, when as 'the greatest jazzman that ever lived' he returned to England to play with the Royal Philharmonic Orchestra at the Royal Festival Hall in aid of the Lord Mayor's National Hungarian and Central European Relief Fund.

When he played his variations of jazz themes he brought back so many memories of my youth and the men who had died in the war.

Now 'Satchmo' the 'iron-lipped trumpeter' was a great lionised star, and everyone knew of his charm, his good-nature, his enormous generosity to charities of every description, and his effort to create good will between the American and British peoples.

When I met him after a superlative show I said:

"Thank you for all you have done for this charity and so many others."

He gave me the grinning smile that was now famous.

"Them that have, gotta give to 'em that haven't, an' I have."

He certainly had!

LADY ASTOR, M.P.

Lady Astor was a very rich woman who never tried to play down her wealth. In 1919 she was the first woman to take her seat in the House of Commons.

In one speech to her constituents she wound up by saying:

"Now, my dears, I'm going back to one of my beautiful palaces to sit down in my tiara and do nothing, and when I roll out in my car I will splash you all with mud and look the other way."

Her audience roared with laughter.

I knew and admired Lady Astor. Who didn't? A Virginian by birth, Protestant and later a Christian Scientist, she was very outspoken and 'Astorisms' became a regular source of amusement. One was never quite certain if she was ingenuous or knew the full value of her remarks.

"I like the common man," she said once, "because I am common myself, but I follow the uncommon man."

On a platform she was fanatical against alcohol, but when I lunched at the Astors' house in St. James's Square with her son he offered me a drink. I looked surprised and he said:

"Mother doesn't approve, but she wants to be hospitable, so our guests have what they want."

It was, however, the most repeated joke of the period when Lady Astor on a platform exclaimed:

"I would rather commit adultery than drink a glass of beer!"

And a man's voice from the back of the hall demanded:

"Who wouldn't?"

It was an extraordinary coincidence that at the time the name of her secretary was Miss Brew!

Lady Astor started the first evening receptions attended only by women. Without drink, without men, they were not surprisingly very dull, and there was no rush for invitations.

At first her fellow Members of Parliament did not take Lady Astor very seriously – a woman in the House of Commons must be a freak – but they grew to respect her, love her for her warm heart, and be infuriated by her unceasing interruptions.

At Cliveden, the Astors' enormous home in Berkshire, Lady Astor only allowed a space of eighteen inches for each guest at the dining table. Any more room she said interrupted good conversation.

Winston Churchill when offered the pudding, said:

She loved being the centre of attraction.

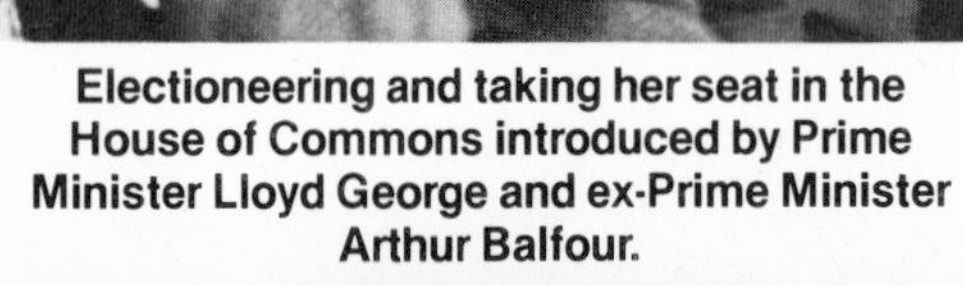

Electioneering and taking her seat in the House of Commons introduced by Prime Minister Lloyd George and ex-Prime Minister Arthur Balfour.

"Take that damned stuff away, I can't move."

At first Lady Astor would not change, but when she learned that at Buckingham Palace each guest had two feet six inches, she gave in.

She had a quick and witty answer for everything, and not only on a platform. When she entered the House of Commons, Winston Churchill, who had known her for a long time, ignored her.

One day she confronted him and asked the reason. He replied that he found a woman's intrusion into the House of Commons as embarrassing as if she burst into his bathroom when he had nothing to defend himself with, but a sponge.

"You are not handsome enough to have worries of that kind!" she replied.

Her Astorisms came thick and fast:

"I would rather be blown up than stuck up."

"I'm no orator and don't want to be – I've heard too many fine phrases from the emptiest heads in Europe."

Provocative, infuriating, at times 'disorderly' she was vital, vivid, compelling, generous, warmhearted, sympathetic, and kind!

When my brother was killed, she wrote to me:

"I feel Ronald will never be away from God. He seemed so near Him."

I think in her own inimitable way that was where Nancy was trying to be.

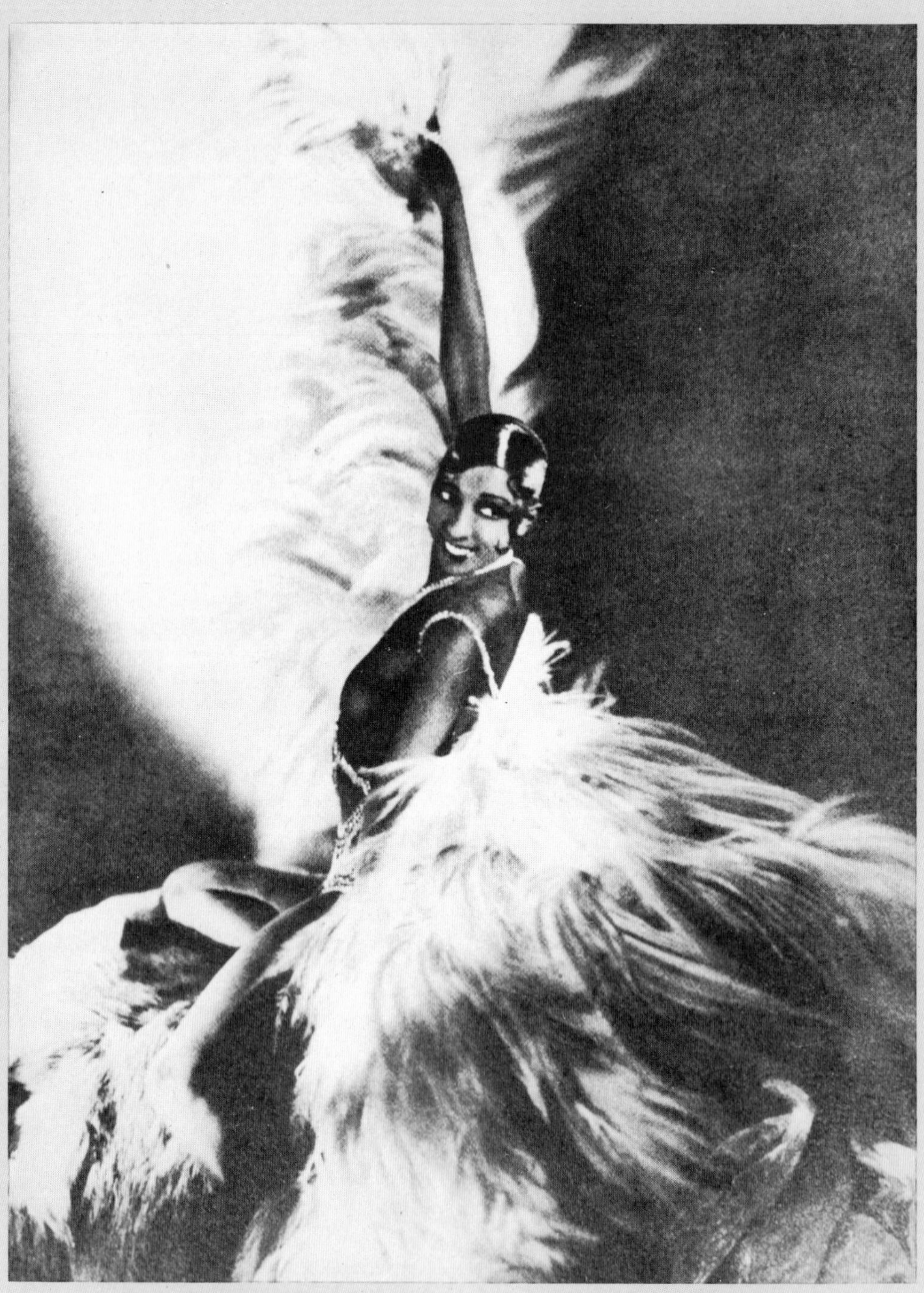

Exotic, exciting, outrageous, provocative, seductive, irresistible! "The Black Venus" swept Paris with her beauty. She was in the 1920s new and sensational and unlike anyone we had seen before!

JOSEPHINE BAKER

When I first met Josephine Baker in Paris in 1925 I didn't dare tell anyone! She was scandalising the capital with her erotic dancing in the *Revue Nègre* at the Théatre de Champs Élysées.

Wearing only a string of imitation bananas round her snake hips, she was declared to be a 'danger to civilisation', and 'a sinuous idol who enslaves and incites all mankind'.

Josephine Baker had been born in a slum in Missouri in 1906 of a Jewish father and a negro mother. She became the first, and certainly the most glamorous, of all the black entertainers who were to follow her.

The appeal of negro art had been steadily growing since 1910, but Josephine Baker was a revolution; the embodiment for the first time of frankly erotic, primitive emotion, although presented with taste and skill.

'The Black Venus', as she was called, had a fire which was so vivid, so intense that she blazed her way into the senses. It was this amazing vitality which enabled her to make her mark in a very different way during World War II.

She served in the Free French Air Force with the rank of Lieutenant, she received the Croix de Guerre and the Rosette de la Résistance, and became a Chevalier de la Légion d'Honneur. She fed and looked after hundreds of war orphans, adopting twelve of them herself.

If she quickened the pulses of the men who applauded her, she also quickened the hearts of those who were prepared to fight and die for freedom.

Lucy Baldwin became almost a national joke. She was robust, forthright, cheerful, friendly, unselfish and good-tempered. She gave Stanley confidence.

With the Cabinet, 1939

Father and Son

STANLEY BALDWIN, M.P.
THE 1st EARL BALDWIN OF BEWDLEY

Prime Minister for eight years, to the Duchess of Windsor "the self-appointed embodiment of John Bull", to Edward VIII the politician who out-manoeuvred him, to the country before the war, a leader who deceived the people in the matter of national defence in order to maintain himself in the office.

My mother saw Stanley Baldwin in another guise. Our families were neighbours in Worcestershire, but she didn't get to know Mr. Baldwin well until after the General Election of 1910.

She and my father went out to Engelburg in Switzerland as guests of the new Member for South Worcestershire, Mr. Eyres Monsell and his wife. In the same hotel was staying Stanley Baldwin, Member for the Bewdley Division, with Mrs. Baldwin and his cousin, Rudyard Kipling.

My mother became firm friends with Stanley Baldwin on the nursery slopes where they were both learning to ski. He never forgot her lighthearted gaiety and the time they spent together.

When Ronald got into the House of Commons they were washing in adjoining basins when Mr. Baldwin told him how he had admired my mother at the Hunt Balls and how everyone wanted to dance with her. He finished by saying:

"Your mother's a wonderful woman!"

It was no surprise that he had an eye for someone pretty because his wife Lucy with her huge over-decorated hats, had become almost a national joke, and one of his biographers says:

"There was not much passion in their mating."

In fact the story which swept the country was that Mrs. Baldwin had said to a friend:

"When Stanley makes love to me I shut my eyes and think of England."

Nevertheless he was a contented middle-class millionaire with a passion for a mechanical piano-player, and a collection of simple jokes which endeared him to his friends.

I however, saw Stanley Baldwin very differently – when Edward VIII said how much the Prime Minister irritated him by nervously cracking and snapping his fingers, I understood.

In 1912 my father arranged a huge Conservative Rally in the grounds of a big house in Pershore. I was ten years old and I walked round the hay-cart which was inevitably the platform at such functions.

Behind it I found a short, stocky, sandy-haired man looking agitated with sweat pouring down his face. When he saw me he started to mop it up rather ineffectively. He seemed to be trembling.

"Are you ill?" I asked.

"It's all right," he replied. "I am always like this before I make a speech. Don't tell anyone."

Following the announcement that Mrs. Simpson's divorce petition was to be heard, King Edward relates in his memoirs how the Prime Minister requested an urgent audience with him at Fort Belvedere.

Mr. Baldwin's colleagues in the Cabinet had been pressing him for a long time to do something about the King's friendship with Mrs. Simpson. They had now insisted that he should ask the King to prevent the divorce from taking place.

Mr. Baldwin arrived at ten o'clock and, although he looked calm and composed, he became restless and finally asked almost apologetically if he might have a whisky and soda.

The King was startled by a request for drink so early in the morning, but I could have explained: Stanley Baldwin was always in 'a nervous state' before he had to speak!

TALLULAH BANKHEAD

The most exciting actress of the Twenties was Tallulah Bankhead. I met her almost as soon as she arrived in London to star in *The Dancers*. She was red-headed, with a smouldering, pouting face. But much more than that, she had a vibrant personality and a strangely arresting voice like hot honey and milk.

She startled all London in 1923. She was 'news' and everyone talked about her. Her entrance into a restaurant was sensational. Old gentlemen told me with shaking voices there had been nothing like it since Lily Langtry.

"Dah-ling," she said to me. "I hear you write plays – write me a really goddam wicked one."

This was not in keeping with her father's idea of Tallulah. I sat next to Senator Bankhead – a white-haired Southern gentleman of the old school – at a dinner party at the Savoy.

"How pretty your daughter is," I remarked.

"Tallulah is just a sweet, pretty gurrl," he replied. "She has high spirits, but there's no harm in that."

Other people were more critical. Hannen Swaffer wrote:

"London would be very dull without Tallulah, especially now Mrs. Meyrick had gone to gaol. We should not have anything to talk about."

Tallulah described herself as 'pure as the driven slush', but Cecil Beaton had other ideas and said:

"She is Medusa, very exotic, with a glorious skull, high pumice-stone cheekbones, and a broad brow."

Tallulah was not only talked about; she was the rage. People amused her, protested against her, but she was electric, compelling, magnetic. When she arrived at a party everyone woke up and it became a noisy success.

She was also very professional. At the first rehearsal for a play Tallulah not only knew her own part but everyone else's part as well.

She was cheerful and she made everyone else cheerful. She was kind, which made her the most popular leading lady in London; even the stage-hands loved her.

But she was always unpredictable. She and Sir Patrick Hastings, who had written a play in which she played the lead, were walking to the theatre after lunching at The Ivy, when a small street-urchin sidled up to them and said:

Tallulah could not resist shocking people by spreading scandalous stories about herself: she also gave cocktail parties in her bath.

She mimicked people, chain-smoke
experimented with drugs.

Tallulah with Godfrey Tearle. One of the great actors of the period. He was so attractive that it was said every man wanted to be a Godfrey Tearle, every woman Gladys Cooper.

Outrageous parties ending in sce
became too outrageous for the Engli
1930 she left for America.

"Stand on me head for sixpence."

"I stand on mine for threepence," Tallulah retorted.

She did! It was lucky that there wasn't much traffic about at the time.

Tallulah was the first person I knew to have fans who screamed as they do today for the pop stars. What was so extraordinary was that they were mostly women. She produced a female mob hysteria which had not been seen before in England.

But she could upstage anyone who upstaged her. Lord Allington, who knew her well, entered a restaurant when she was dining, with his mother. He chose to ignore Tallulah.

A few minutes later she walked up to his table.

"My Lord does not recognise me," she asked sweetly, "with my clothes on?"

Max's description of himself was:
"I am the victim of the Furies. On the rockbou
coast of New Brunswick the waves break
incessantly. Every now and then comes a
particularly dangerous wave smashing viciou
against the rock. It is called The Rage. That's n

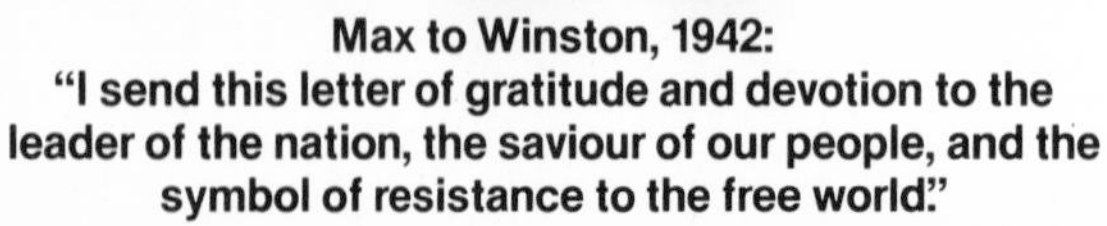

Max to Winston, 1942:
"I send this letter of gratitude and devotion to the leader of the nation, the saviour of our people, and the symbol of resistance to the free world."

LORD BEAVERBROOK

Lady Diana Cooper described Lord Beaverbrook as 'a strange attractive gnome with the odour of genius about him'.

To me he exuded the unmistakable vitality of success which seemed to vibrate in the air around him.

In 1923 I was trying to write a novel in between dancing all night. At a party I met a young reporter on the *Daily Express* who suggested I should contribute to the Gossip Column which had become an important feature on the paper.

He said he would pay me 5s. a paragraph which was to me a lot of money and I felt I was rich!

After I had written for the *Daily Express* a few months and also contributed several articles which brought me in two or three guineas a time, the telephone rang and I was told that Lord Beaverbrook would like to see me.

A car was sent for me to go to a small, unimpressive house called 'The Vineyards', near Hurlingham.

I thought when I first saw him, he looked like a lucky talisman we had carried in the war – the God of Good Luck – called 'Billikens'. He was certainly very lucky for me for he taught me how to write, and I believe it is entirely due to him that I have been so successful with my books and the thousands of articles I have done over the years.

Max was fascinating because he seemed omnipotent, enigmatic, and had a strange dynamic vitality which was mesmeric, but he was human with many frailties.

No one had been impressed when he bought the *Daily Express* at the end of the war for the sum of £17,500. In fact, his friends told him that he had wasted his money, and any more that he poured into the newspaper would be 'buried in Fleet Street'.

But the *Daily Express* fully expressed the ebullient, relentless, mission-laden personality of its owner, and it became the most widely-read daily newspaper in the world.

Max was forty-four when I met him, and although it took me time to discover it, he was passing through a particularly difficult and unhappy period of his life.

Bonar Law, the 'unknown Prime Minister' to whom he had been private secretary and whom he had loved, had died, and Max said to me once, almost savagely:

"Do you know what it's like to watch someone you know dying slowly, day by day, to know that you cannot help them, that you can do nothing for them? Have you any idea what it's like to sit there wanting to give them a part of yourself, a part of your life, some of the years you still have to live, and knowing you are helpless?"

Another time he said to me of Bonar Law:

"He would have been the greatest Prime Minister we've ever had, but – he died in my arms."

I didn't know then how Bonar Law had once tried to take his own life when he had retired to the South of France.

It was before he knew he had cancer of the throat and he sent for Max, or rather he told him what he had tried to do, and Max abandoned everything to go to help his friend, but was still powerless.

"I watched a man die!"

He was to say it over and over again because it had happened just a few months before I came into his life.

Years later when I wrote the story of Metternich the great Austrian Statesman, who all his life had searched for the ecstasy he had felt in his first love-affair, I thought of Max.

The two men were totally unlike each other in every way, except they both had the same magnetic power and both searched for a perfect, ideal love they knew once.

Max, I am convinced, measured all men he met by what he had felt for Bonar Law. When sometimes he believed in them for a short while and they failed him, he hated them because they had revived within him the hope that he would once again love and trust a man who would become for him, another hero.

But Max was too vital a person to spend his life looking back into the past.

He never told me what an important part he had played in politics or about the magnificent job he performed in war propaganda for the Canadian Forces.

One tribute to his success in comparison to other propagandists was shown in the *Punch* cartoon of someone asking a British Tommy:

"Why do we never hear what you are doing?"

"Oh, I only appear on the casualty lists," was the answer.

Max had stood as a Parliamentary candidate for Ashton-under-Lyne – a Manchester seat. He was a stranger to England and he had only ten days to win the seat for the Liberals. His opponent was a local man. Max got in with a majority of 196.

His new triumph however, seemed at first a cul-de-sac. He was not liked in the House of Commons. Like other great reformers he was too dynamic for that mellow complacent atmosphere.

Max learnt to speak, he studied politics and politicians, he studied England and the English with his perceptive superhuman concentration. By 1923 he became a power but he never tried to popularise himself. He was content to pull the strings with others gaining the acclamations.

He was always looking forward, trying out the new, attempting to change the traditional and the conventional in both big things and small.

Just before I met him he employed craftsmen who were making him new designs in furniture. With his money he could have bought the most fabulous treasures in the world, but instead he encouraged a few obscure workmen to create for him something no one else possessed.

When I met him he had suddenly come to the decision that he should know more about music.

As 'The Vineyards' was very small, the musicians who played oboes, harps, cellos and violins were usually forced to do so in the garden. Although they did their best, the conversation was usually so interesting that nobody listened to the poor players.

I remember a night when a Russian choir had arrived in England to be met at Southampton and rushed by car to 'The Vineyards' to sing at a dinner party of eight.

As they stepped into the dining room Max, in one of his most puckish moods, had a film of Russian life taken immediately after the Revolution thrown on to the wall behind his chair.

It was a propaganda film and there were various horrifying close-up shots of children crawling with lice and dying of starvation.

The Russians, who could not speak English, were stunned, as well they might have been and Lord Birkenhead whispered to me:

"We'll all get a knife in our backs at any moment!"

As is inevitable with anyone as vital as Max, people disparaged his arrogance, his impetuosity, his ruthlessness, his impatience, his intolerance and his habit which increased as he grew older, of sucking a person dry, like an orange, and chucking them aside.

But his perceptive, microscopic mind was always looking towards new horizons.

His worst fault was that to those he disliked he was vindictive to the point of absurdity.

The two men he tried to destroy for no apparent reason were Anthony Eden and Lord Mountbatten. He used all his power as a Press Baron against them, his newspapers were instructed to attack and disparage them continually.

Later Max was polished in a great many ways by the Honourable Mrs. Richard Norton who was one of the great beauties of the Twenties, and who really loved him.

But in 1924 he let his valet buy his clothes at Harrods which were rather badly fitting, nondescript navy-blue suits, and his shoes, bought in the same way, had thick soles.

He was also at that time, though he changed over the years, indifferent to food and wine.

His two great friends, Lord Birkenhead and Winston Churchill, were always complaining:

"Where did you get this claret, Max?"

"The grocer's, I think."

"It tastes like it!"

Max had been horribly teased as a boy about his looks until while playing with the idea of everything around him being beautiful he was not interested in himself. Yet he said to me:

"A man wants to spread his tail like a peacock!"

He had been deprived of love in his childhood and I think what he remembered most was wanting to escape, of being ashamed of being so poor, although later he used to boast about it.

One thing he told me, which was very revealing, was about a big dance which was held in Newcastle, New Brunswick.

Max, young, ambitious and studying Law, wanted to be present. He was told by a friend that as a Law Student he would get an invitation.

He hired a tail-coat, white shirt and tie and waited. He told me how finally he contacted his friend and complained he had not yet received the precious card which would admit him.

"I'm sorry," his friend replied, "you can't go after all. They have learned that in the past you sold newspapers in the streets. We cannot have newsboys at this Assembly."

I knew by his voice how much it had hurt him.

"What did you do?" I asked.

"I went home," Max replied, "and put on that dress-suit. I stood in front of a mirror. I looked at my reflection and I said to myself: 'The day will come when they'll be glad to ask me to their goddamned Assembly!' "

That was the secret!

When Max was made Minister of Supply in 1941, Privy Seal, Lend-Lease Administrator to the U.S.A., and Chancellor of the University of New Brunswick in 1947, he was still showing that 'goddamned Assembly' exactly what they had missed.

THE 1st EARL OF BIRKENHEAD
F. E. SMITH

Tall, very dark, athletic, he had an olive skin, heavy-lidded eyes, a disdainful imperious manner, and was so overwhelming that one could understand how he dominated every Court in which he appeared.

I met Lord Birkenhead, who was always called F.E., with Max Beaverbrook.

He was fascinating, witty, charming when he wished to be, but he was a man who could be inscrutably stern, aggressive, sarcastic. He had in fact destroyed his own political chances by antagonising the Junior Ministers, by lecturing them in a manner which made them more indignant with every brow-beating sentence he spoke.

Max told me that Bonar Law used to quote an Arab Proverb which was very appropriate to F.E.:

Easier to keep a live coal in the mouth than a witty saying.

Judges never got the better of him. One, after a long legal wrangle on a point of procedure, asked him sarcastically:

"Whatever do you suppose I am on the Bench for, Mr. Smith?"

"It is not for me, M'Lud, to attempt to fathom the inscrutable workings of Providence," was the reply.

He once, however, lost a great sum of money by being witty. Robert Houston, a wealthy Lancashire ship-owner, promised to make him one of his heirs. Sir Robert was very proud of his red beard, which, as he got older kept its original colour. He was also a right-wing die-hard Tory.

At a dinner party someone mentioned Sir Robert and F.E. remarked:

"Of course, he's the original dye-hard."

It was an expensive joke: Sir Robert cut him out of his will.

He could also be bluntly and extremely rude when irritated. One night a truculent feminist, determined to pick an argument, exclaimed:

"You're impossible F.E.! You don't even talk to me like a gentleman!"

"Talk to you like a gentleman! My dear Lady —," he replied, "you wouldn't understand me if I did."

F.E. had made a memorable remark in his Electoral Address at Glasgow University when he said:

"The world continues to offer glittering prizes to those who have stout hearts and sharp swords."

But it was his sharp tongue which made him many enemies even

F.E. adored the *Mairi*. At Cowes with his wife, younger daughter Pamela, Field Marshall Lord Allenby, and Sir John Simon.

F.E. never swerved in devoted and sacrificing friendship for Churchill. He had the more brilliant mind — Winston the stronger character. In public he was cynical and flippant. To his colleagues a loyal, unselfish friend with nerves of steel in times of stress and danger.

though his charm and kindness won him many loyal friends.

I have never seen anyone take so much exercise as F.E. I was in a house-party with him once when he played thirty-six holes of golf in the morning, after lunch he rode for two hours on tricky rampageous little Scottish ponies, then he played three sets of tennis and when everyone was exhausted, asked if anyone would like another round of golf before dinner.

At Cowes he would work off some of his energy in the sea. His favourite trick was to dive from his yacht the *Mairi* with a lighted cigar in his mouth, then come to the surface with it still alight.

I think he liked me because I stood up to him. Once we had what might be called a row. He was, I thought, pursuing a pretty but very empty-headed friend of mine.

With what seems to me now incredible, if impertinent, courage I tackled him, saying passionately:

"It's not fair! Any great brain can subdue a lesser. You know that! You could make anyone do anything you wanted and certainly make V— fall in love with you!"

F.E. was sitting in front of the fire, his long legs stretched out in front of him. He took his cigar out of his mouth to say distinctly:

"You go to blazes!"

I knew I had convinced him. We sat in silence for a long time. Then suddenly he smiled at me.

"You know, Barbara," he said, "I shall be very interested to see what you make of your career."

F.E. liked ostentation and he could never keep money.

He had three cars all painted yellow, his stables were filled with horses, some of which he had never ridden, but he loved his yacht *Mairi* more than any of them.

He could see no good in an enemy, no bad in a friend. He hated as passionately as he loved.

He was intensely proud of being what I called him – an Adventurer. He certainly resembled a character from the pages of Dumas. He was brave – but terrified of going to the dentist.

In October 1924, soon after I met F.E., there was a General Election, which followed the exposure of the Zinoviev letter.

The Conservatives swept the country and F.E. was appointed Secretary of State for India under the leadership of Stanley Baldwin, who had become Prime Minister.

F.E. invited me to a great and glittering reception he gave at the India Office that summer. It was a spectacle I shall never forget. I was thrilled by the beauty and pageantry of the Indian women in their vivid saris and by the jewelled turbans of the Indian Princes.

My own pleasure was somewhat marred by the fact that I was the only woman present without gloves. They were so rarely worn in the careless Twenties that on this auspicious occasion I never thought of them.

On another occasion F.E. asked me to go with him to a dinner which was being given for the most discussed and most popular play of the time, *The Constant Nymph*.

It was to run for two years to a packed theatre and Margaret Kennedy became a celebrity.

"You write too," F.E. said to me. "You had better come to dinner with me and see I do it right."

Proudly I accompanied the greatest orator of the day. He told me he had had a long and trying session in the House of Lords and he drained a large glass of brandy before we set off. It was obviously not the first.

From a seat in the centre of the hall I watched F.E. at the top table and thought nervously he seemed sleepy and uncommunicative.

Finally he rose to speak. He made a brilliant, clear, concise and very flattering oration. Unfortunately he took as his subject H.G. Wells and never once mentioned Margaret Kennedy!

It was only later that I began to realise that he was a disappointed man.

His brain was so brilliant, he had a photographic memory, and he would have had tremendous powers of leadership if he had ever been able to control his tongue and to 'suffer fools gladly'. But this was really impossible for him.

He had, moreover, become Lord Chancellor, the highest legal post in the British Isles, when he was only forty-seven. I think he dreamt of greater horizons and was always disappointed that he could not reach them.

He was not a spiritually-minded man, but he could be warm and sentimental although his enemies were not to know this.

As Lord Chancellor he had worked as no other man in that particular post had ever worked before or since, and it was said of him that he was 'the greatest Judge who ever sat on the Wool-sack'. Yet apart from positions like being Secretary of State for India there was no chance of his going higher still.

It was impossible in those days to consider having a Prime Minister who was in the House of Lords.

Lord Wavertree had a new interest at that time in astrology. He had a friend, I imagine impoverished, who cast all our horoscopes.

I was staying at Cherkley, Lord Beaverbrook's house in the country, when F.E. received his.

He read it to me. It said: "You will have one more great rise, then a great fall."

"I cannot imagine what the great rise will be," he said, and there was no mistaking the bitterness in his voice, "unless of course a grateful people make me King!"

JACK BUCHANAN

I met the most glamorous man of the period in the early Thirties when we presented the prizes at 'The Servants Ball' which was held at Harrods. I doubt if we could fill a ballroom with that elusive race today!

Handsome, debonair, nonchalant in his top hat and tails, he was the personification of every girl's ideal hero, and he was a superb dancer with a natural ability for acting.

So many songs of the period bring him vividly back to my mind: *Her Mother Came Too*, *Who?*, *I'm in a Dancing Mood*, and especially *Fancy Our Meeting*.

Jack believed that the public had a right to expect exemplary behaviour and a well-dressed appearance from its stars, and he would say to the members of his company:

"If you want to wear your old woollens and slacks go home, but you must always dress up both to go out on the town and when going to and from the theatre."

He, himself, was known as London's best-dressed man. His suits were made by Hawes & Curtis, his dressing gowns by Turnbull & Asser, his shoes by Lobb, his famous grey trilby by Herbert Johnson.

He invented the backless evening-waistcoat and in 1924 appeared in the first double-breasted dinner-jacket in *Toni* at the Shaftesbury Theatre.

He was overwhelmingly generous to anyone who appealed to him for help. In fact they called him 'the softest touch in show-business'.

When an old school friend, John Logie Baird, told Jack he was having difficulty in arousing any interest in his new invention – the television – Jack introduced him to the right people and backed him.

At the luncheon on 1 May 1925 Jack said:

"When the system is perfected we should be able to see the finish of the Derby, or any other topical event, in our own homes at the moment of occurrence."

Jack lost a lot of money on television, especially in America, but he believed in it and he pioneered it.

He was a huge draw in the films, but the stage was his real love. "I'm very sensitive to audiences," he said often, and he would woo them until they were in the right mood.

In 1956 tests showed he had cancer of the spine but he continued to work as hard as ever. His last professional appearance, given by sheer

Apart from his handsome glamorous appearance Jack was a perfect broadcaster. He sounded unafraid unruffled, perfectly natural with a most sympathetic singing voice. Actually he was a mass of nerves

Jack in the first dinner-jacket in 1924.

Elsie Randolph was a perfect partner for Jack. The most famous, however, now known to millions over the world, was Anna Neagle.

willpower and determination, was appearing as principal guest artist at the opening of Scottish I.T.V.

He appeared, inevitably in top hat, white tie and tails, to perform some of his best-known numbers. He was so brilliant that the reviewers wrote of his prospects in more films and plays.

Jack died peacefully in 1957 and his wife Suzzie said:

"We crammed a lifetime of happiness into nine short, wonderful years of marriage."

For me like all those who remember him so elegant, glamorous, professionally perfect, so irresistibly charming on or off the stage, he was, as in the last lines of *Fancy Our Meeting*, which became his theme song – 'a dream worth dreaming come true'.

With the converted at the Oxford Group.

With Bunny Austin, the tennis star.

DR. FRANK BUCHMANN

I met Dr. Frank Buchmann at Dr. Dengler's Clinic at Baden-Baden. Granted that people are not at their best when they are taking liver-salts and dieting for one reason or another, still I was disappointed.

An American, he had inaugurated the Oxford Group Movement, which had an amazing success in the Twenties. After a vision of the Cross in England in 1908 he believed he had discovered within himself a new power.

He began to change the lives of his friends. House-parties were arranged all over England where he spoke and those present 'shared' their sins.

The Group started in the English Universities but extended their message to industries and coal mines.

Their aims were:

Absolute poverty
Absolute purity
Absolute unselfishness
Absolute love.

The Marquess of Salisbury – one of the most influential men in Britain – was one of Dr. Buchmann's supporters.

When asked why, he replied:

"It is the spirit moving on the water, and I dare not stand aside."

Criticism abounded because in surrendering themselves to the Movement the Groups were also asked to surrender their money. Moreover they published no accounts, and when asked why when travelling they stayed in 'posh' hotels Dr. Buchmann replied:

"Why shouldn't we stay in posh hotels? Isn't God a millionaire?"

At this time Lord Salisbury said in the House of Lords:

"If I may use a phrase which is common in a Great Movement which is taking place at this moment in this country and elsewhere, what you want are God-guided personalities which make God-guided nationalities, to make a new world."

Buchmann had many important followers. The Earl of Athlone made a broadcast on 'Moral Rearmament', which the Oxford Movement came to be called. Mahatma Gandhi and Dr. Sun Yat-sen of China became Buchmann's friends. While the Bishop of London, Dr.

Winnington-Ingram, sent Sir Lyndon Macassey, when he was leader of the Parliamentary Bar and later head of Reuters, to examine his work. Both subsequently supported him for the rest of his life.

In Baden-Baden I asked Dr. Buchmann to hold a meeting at the Sanatorium in the evening, so that we could ask him questions. He was rather reluctant, but I pressed him and he agreed.

About thirty people attended. Dr. Buchmann was stocky, stout and benevolent-looking, with thin smiling lips and bright eyes behind gold-rimmed spectacles.

One would have guessed him to be a Bank Manager. I asked a number of questions which he answered accurately but uninspiringly. It was difficult to understand why he had such success.

His enemies were violently opposed to the Movement. A fellow and tutor of an Oxford College wrote:

> I have known Oxford for three years as an under-graduate and I have worked in Oxford as a College Tutor for some twenty-two years; it seems to me that of all the movements almost if not quite the most depraved in its attitude, tending to be most insidiously inimical to the formation of fine character, is the Group Movement which Dr. Buchmann has brought us from America.

Yet thousands of people, including Royalty like Queen Marie of Romania, the ex-King George of Greece, and the King of Spain, followed him in admiration.

I wanted to feel the vivid spark which he ignited in them. I felt nothing.

As the meeting broke up a friend with me said:

"Wouldn't it be awful if when we get to Heaven we find Frank Buchmann is God!"

GEORGES CARPENTIER

On 4 December 1919 I was taken to the Holborn Stadium by two young men to see the Carpentier–Beckett fight when the gate money of £30,000 broke all records.

There was great excitement about the fight, as the Frenchman, Georges Carpentier, was extremely good-looking with slender muscles and an adolescent silhouette, contrasting strangely with Joe Beckett with his battered nose, enormous jaw, square chin and deep set eyes.

But Beckett was undoubtedly the favourite!

It was very unusual in those days for a lady, especially a debutante, to attend a fight, but my young men wanted to give me a treat, and I didn't like to dampen their ardour by saying I didn't want to go.

Tickets were more precious than gold, as Olympia was being done up and couldn't be used, and the Holborn Stadium only held five thousand seats, so thousands were unable to get in.

The Prince of Wales was present, and when Carpentier appeared there were roars of "*Allez Georges!*", "*Allez France!*"

As soon as the men started to fight it was obvious that Carpentier was light and agile on his feet – Beckett slow and heavy.

Suddenly, so quickly that I felt it couldn't have happened, Carpentier let fly with a right hook. There was a dull sound, then Beckett raised his arms and crashed to the ground like a fallen tree.

It was all over in three minutes!!

Two years later in 1921 I followed Georges Carpentier's fight with Jack Dempsey with the greatest interest. He lost, but with such courage that he won the esteem and affection of the whole of America!

At the time Carpentier was often in England, staying with Sir Philip Sassoon. He carried a cigarette-case with the signatures on it of Admiral Beatty, Winston Churchill, Lloyd George, Lord Birkenhead and Lord Montagu. (Not a bad collection for a Frenchman!)

When Eamonn Andrews interviewed me in the programme *This is Your Life* in 1958, the B.B.C. flew Georges Carpentier from France to meet me and Eamonn said to him:

"Wasn't it quite a new thing in 1919 for ladies to watch boxing?"

"In those days perhaps it was," Carpentier replied, "but it was always evening-dress at the ringside, you know, and boxing had become a fashionable sport."

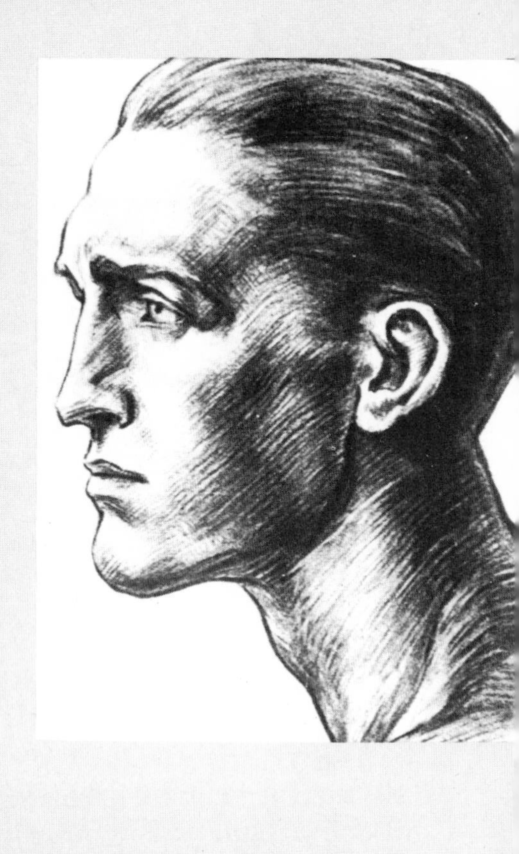

Georges Carpentier with me doing *This is Your Life* in 1958, with Eamonn Andrews. It was a great surprise! In those days as 'the victim' I was not allowed to speak!

Georges was almost the first boxer, with his gre skill and strength, to attract women to a sport hitherto considered brutalising.

"You were something of a social lion too, Georges."

"People were very kind," Carpentier smiled, "and I enjoyed myself. I met many charming people over here; and I think of my visits with great affection. Ladies like Miss Cartland made me realise that, despite the war, England still retained something of the old elegance."

"We were all in love with you," I told him as he kissed my hand.

Wine and beautiful women.

"Had I behaved respectably," he said, "I should have died rich. Alas! I am turning somersaults and chucking 'Aunt Sallies' at life."

Cigars and Churchill.

Valentine with his beautiful and tempestuous wife Doris.

VISCOUNT CASTLEROSSE

Viscount Castlerosse, an Irish aristocrat and the most brilliant wit of the period, was so strange to look at, so extraordinary in his habits that he would have been an eccentric in any age in which he lived.

He had had an unhappy childhood. He believed that his mother, whom he adored, preferred his brother Dermot because he was so much better-looking.

"I was an ugly, awkward child," he said. "My feet were too small for my body, I was frightened of heights, I was slow of speech and I blushed a lot. I believed that she was always thinking: 'What a shame Dermot isn't the heir.' "

When Dermot was killed in 1915 his mother never recovered. Valentine tried to comfort her, but he was coldly repulsed.

"It was obvious to me," he said, "that my mother was thinking: 'Why should he be alive when Dermot is dead?' "

This started the complexes which were to affect Castlerosse all his life. The fact that he felt himself to be ugly and unwanted made it inevitable that he would believe that women didn't like him.

Because he was ashamed of having no love-affairs he invented them, telling wild, improbable tales to his fellow undergraduates at Cambridge of what dashing things he had done in the presence of some entirely mythical young woman.

He hated the Army and its routine, which was perhaps not surprising, but it merely added to his sense of inferiority.

A luncheon which took place by chance because Lord Birkenhead happened to ask Castlerosse as one of his guests was to be a turning-point in his life. When the war was over he and Max Beaverbrook became close – and to other people incomprehensibly – friends.

Castlerosse's loneliness was in some way relieved. With Max he could relax and unburden himself. During the years together they would often have violent rows. Castlerosse got into every sort of trouble, usually financial, but Max always paid and paid and paid.

But one thing the years of frustration had produced in Valentine was an insatiable appetite for eating and drinking. Today any psychiatrist could explain it by the fact that Castlerosse wanted love, but perhaps he wanted it more greedily than anyone else had done before.

He was a colossal eater. I have watched him, fascinated, eating enough food to satisfy a man and a woman for a week, and at the end he would say he was still hungry.

"I don't know how it started," Valentine said, "except that suddenly I began to get hungrier and hungrier. I found I needed vast quantities of food to sustain me, and my thirst for alcoholic liquids was practically unquenchable. I do not think that even my worst enemy can say that it has affected the quickness of my mind – just the bloody opposite, in fact."

In 1924 Valentine was easily one of the most spectacular figures in London, his enormous chest enveloped in a purple overcoat, his small feet swathed in spats, the gold watch-chain across the ever-increasing stomach.

His uncle, Lord Revelstoke, known as the 'Emperor of Finance', arranged for him to work with a firm of stockbrokers in the City, but he hated the job and he hated the people.

"There is nothing more boring than money in the Bank," he said, "especially if it belongs to someone else."

He began to arrive later and later at the office, until finally one of his friends remonstrated with him.

"It is a disgrace how late you come in, Valentine!"

"But think how early I go!" Castlerosse replied.

Shortly after this his services were no longer needed.

I remember Castlerosse sitting at luncheon stuffing food into himself, and making us all roar with laughter as he told the story of how he had gone to the Savoy to lunch with Lord Birkenhead.

"We had an excellent meal," he said, "I was on my way to the cloakroom, a cigar in my mouth and my hand in my pocket struggling to get my matches, when my fingers encountered some papers. I pulled them out. Just then somebody bumped into me and they fell to the floor right at the foot of a gentleman whom I recognised as an official of my uncle's firm. He bent down to help me pick up what I had dropped, and handed me back my papers with a knowing and triumphant smile. I recognised them too: they were £20,000 of National War Bonds which I had stuffed into my pocket absent-mindedly and taken with me out to lunch."

Castlerosse took another huge mouthful of food.

"It did not need the mind of a genius," he continued, "to know that once the tale reached my uncle my career as a stockbroker would be at an end. I went back into the dining room, drank another brandy, while the official of my uncle's firm – a gentleman much given to licking the boots of his superiors – scuttled back to the City with his titbit of scandal. Then with the leisurely calm of a man who has no more to lose I followed."

Once inside the office Castlerosse went straight to his uncle's room and walked in. He threw the bonds down on Lord Revelstoke's desk.

"Greetings, dear Uncle," he said genially. "And how's the old bucket-shop doing today?"

It might have been funny to us, but it was definitely the end of

Lady Diana Cooper

In an echo from the past Diana as a nun at a fancy dress ball with Lord Goodman — the famous solicitor — dressed as a monk.

Diana aged 20 in 1912 — love-in-the-mist eyes, a translucent skin, pale gold hair with the delicate texture of Chinese silk, she lit a room with her "flawless awe-inspiring beauty."

Diana Cooper, the most beautiful woman in the world with a radiance, an inner glow of unquenchable vitality, with Noel Coward whose infinite charm, brilliant talents and kind heart made him unique.

Noel Coward

Noel the victor — the Master! But who understood the real Noel?
"One's real inside self is a private place," he said, "and should always stay like that. It is no one else's business."

Noel alone.
"World of strange enchantment..."
Dreaming of the future, reaching for the Crown.
"Overture Beginners — Everybody Down."*
*Not yet the Dodo.

Castlerosse's career in the City, and he fell desperately into debt. Max paid again!

Valentine was his Court Jester. He would sit gorging himself with food and drink, apparently not even listening to the conversation, until Max would say:

"What do you think about it, Valentine?"

It was the cue for the song he must sing for his supper. Castlerosse would look up at the ceiling and without a pause give a quick, spontaneous, witty reply. I never knew him fail the challenge.

In 1926 Max had a brainwave. In April the *Sunday Express* announced a new departure in Sunday journalism.

> The London Log will in future be edited and signed by Viscount Castlerosse.

Valentine's page was a success from the very moment he started writing. It was clever, witty, indiscreet, and full of names we all knew. Everyone in the social world snatched the *Sunday Express* as soon as it appeared on Sunday morning and read Castlerosse before they even looked at the headlines.

The readers loved the way he lampooned the pompous leaders of society. They liked the impression he gave of always being in the know, of being able to say a great deal more if he dared, but even so, managing to give them spicy human titbits about people who before had just been mere names.

My favourite story of those which Valentine told about himself was when he went to the Arts Ball in Paris dressed like one of Attila's Huns, wearing only a few skins. When he returned half-naked to his hotel, he met an elderly maiden lady in the corridor.

"My God!" she ejaculated.

"Yes, Madam," Valentine replied, "but tonight strictly incognito."

Then just as it seemed that Valentine had found a special niche for himself, and some of his feelings of insecurity and inadequacy were disappearing, he fell in love with the most temperamental, extravagant, arrogant, and beautiful woman in London. Her name was Doris Delavigne.

Doris had been seen around Mayfair for some time before she met Valentine in 1928.

She had been born in 1900 in Streatham, and Michael Arlen was reputed to have used her as a model for the heroine of *The Green Hat* – actually there were few pretty women he wasn't supposed to have used. Noel Coward certainy copied her in *Private Lives*, using her language, her outlook, her appearance and behaviour.

Elinor Glyn once said to me: "She lookes like a hungry fox!" But most people compared Doris to 'a nervous and sensitive deer, possessing the grace and ferocity of a panther'.

Doris really was beautiful. There was not a man who saw her and didn't feel attracted to her. She had perfect legs, a wonderful figure, and a skin which had some strange quality about it – once a man had touched it he could never forget. And yet she had a viper's tongue.

She had a vocabulary which left people open-mouthed, and which not unnaturally shocked into silence the majority of those who heard her speak her mind.

Because she was beautiful, because she was outrageous, because she gave the impression of not caring whether people liked her or not, Doris became the rage.

She had once been madly in love with a Polo-playing American who had 'ditched' her for a married woman, as beautiful as Doris but with the advantages of great wealth and an unassailable social background.

Doris was certainly deeply seared by the experience. It changed her character, made her hard and cynical, although she was always in many ways good-natured.

Men fought to take her out, and it gave them a certain prestige to be seen dining in her company. She attracted men, from Guards Officers to Statesmen and politicians, and it was inevitable that to get into Society she would want to marry someone of importance.

The last thing anyone expected, either for her or for Valentine Castlerosse, was that they would marry each other.

They fought from the very beginning. One would see them together at the Embassy Club: Doris's eyes would be flashing and Valentine would be more crimson in the face than usual. Sometimes she would get up and walk out of the Club, leaving him alone, spluttering with fury over his piled plate.

After a moment his big fat hand would go out to grasp the neck of a bottle, and he would pour himself another drink.

His friends tried to make Castlerosse see sense.

"You are making a fool of yourself, Valentine!" one of these said in my presence.

"I can't help myself," Valentine answered in a desperate voice. "I am not just in love, I'm infatuated, obsessed, bewitched! I can't live without her."

Everybody in London knew the story of Doris telling a friend of Castlerosse how badly she was being treated. She showed him the mass of bruises on her white arms.

"You had better warn him as a friend," she said, "that if he behaves like this again I shall inform the police. Meanwhile you can make him return the key of my house: he is not coming in any more."

The friend found Valentine and gave him the message.

"How dare she say such a thing!" he exclaimed.

He rolled up his trouser-leg and displayed a bandaged calf.

"Look what she has done to me, with her teeth, too."

Everyone agreed that it would be ridiculous and insane for Doris and

Valentine to be married. Max Beaverbrook begged Castlerosse to be sensible, and Valentine promised him over and over again that he would leave her alone.

Valentine tried to forget his misery in an orgy of drinking and eating. His waistline expanded, and so did his debts. But he made up his mind. On 28 May 1928 at 10.30 a.m. he and Doris were married at Hammersmith Register Office.

It was, as everybody had forecast, a disastrous and unhappy marriage. They fought in private, they fought in public, yet some strange inexplicable magic drew them back to each other.

They lived at Doris's house which was opposite mine in Culross Street. One morning very early, I happened to look out of my window and I saw an enormous Falstaffian figure in blue silk pyjamas walking angrily up and down the pavement, crimson with rage, spluttering with anger and muttering to himself.

It was Valentine, who after one of his rows with Doris had been locked out!

The rest of the story is even more bizarre.

Valentine decided to get a divorce. His detectives reported that Doris had been traced to the Ritz Hotel in Paris where she was with a man.

They telephoned Valentine and he replied:

"Yes, she has a man with her, but you bloody fools, it's me!"

After ten years of marriage they were finally divorced in 1938. Doris, unbelievably, became very close friends with an exceedingly rich American woman.

When the war started Doris went to America. In 1942 she met Winston Churchill there and he told her to return to England.

She called Valentine on her arrival and they dined that night at the Dorchester.

She suggested he should marry her – he refused. A week or so later she died of an overdose of sleeping-pills.

Stricken by the tragedy Valentine wrote in a long letter to Beaverbrook:

> There is no logic in love. I loved Doris with a folly and a futility that passes belief . . . I could have lifted her up and given her hope but I did not. I let her die and all because for once I was going to be wise . . .
>
> There is a tremendous force in the world and it is love – and I loved Doris.

Three weeks later Valentine married again and in a few months he too was dead of heart failure.

So much wit, entertainment and uninhibited laughter died with him. He was a great jester who was always hungry for love.

Winston electioneering with verve.

Winston with my brother Ronald, the first Member of Parliament to be killed in 1940. Winston loved him.

Painting.

Arriving at the Admiralty in 1939.

SIR WINSTON CHURCHILL

The most interesting person I met with Lord Beaverbrook was, of course, his greatest and closest friend, Winston Churchill.

It was impossible when he was present not to find oneself watching and listening to him. Before he arrived the others would say:

"I suppose we shall have to listen to that endless tirade from Winston about the next war that is to come!"

Yet when he talked they still listened although they had heard it before.

To me he had a magic which was inescapable, which my brother found when he entered the House of Commons in 1935. Winston Churchill befriended him and gave him an affection which was an inspiration and a guidance that he followed until he was killed.

It was not so much what Winston Churchill said.

It was the irresistible Churchill magnetism which gave him a kind of aura which showed itself from the moment he was born to the moment he died.

In 1924 he had been through a very bad time. He was without a Parliamentary seat and when he lost in Manchester the Stock Exchange telegraphed him jeeringly:

What is the use of a W.C. without a seat?

As always when Winston was up against it he was very voluble in defence of himself.

He was not defeated; he was undefeatable, and yet he had been hurt in knowing his brilliance was unappreciated and that his political acumen had not more support in the country. But as usual he was looking ahead and prophesying.

I remember him holding the table and saying positively the Socialist Government would not last and the Liberals would inevitably withdraw their support from Ramsay MacDonald's administration.

Sparks seemed to fly from him as he spoke, and if I watched wide-eyed, so did his friends even though they teased him.

But he had that capacity for concentrating on what he was doing to the exclusion of all else.

When he was staying at Cherkley he set up his easel in the garden and started to paint the shrubs on the terrace. He had been taught to paint by the lovely Lady Lavery when he was miserable and at a loose end, having lost office during the First World War.

He had bought a canvas but he really didn't know what to do with it. Lady Lavery, who was an artist like her husband, took his brush, mixed the paints and showed him how to apply them.

He seemed to me to be depicting the shrubs in very strange colours.

"Why have you made that bush purple?" I asked.

"That's how I see it," he growled. "And that is how it is!"

It was only much later in life that I found that very vital people like vital colours, and perhaps because their senses are so highly attuned they see everything more vividly than duller nondescript personalities.

In those days he did not always have a cigar in his mouth and it was Max who later revealed in his book *Men and Power* that it was something of a pose. Max wrote:

"He appeared to smoke cigars incessantly. Not at all. He smoked very little, although re-lighting a cigar frequently, his use of matches outstripped his consumption of cigars."

Perhaps because Max, Winston and F.E. were all so famous, when people write of them they eulogise over their achievements, the great things they did for the world, their ambitions and the endeavours of their lives, and make them sound almost inhuman.

I like to remember their sense of humour. Winston would laugh until the tears ran down his cheeks.

F.E. would tell anecdote after anecdote, not the spiteful, bitter ones that made him so many quite unnecessary enemies at the Bar and in the House of Commons, but gay, amusing stories and often against himself.

Max would seldom tell tales, but he would laugh and manipulate the conversation. He could make it good-humoured or serious at will, and he knew it.

And for me, I can look back and see them sitting in the dull beige-coloured room at 'The Vineyards', with its low ceiling and inadequate lighting from the small windows.

I can hear Winston oratorically sincere, passionate and as determined to convince us that he was right as if he was speaking to thousands of people at the Albert Hall.

Beside him F.E., scintillating, sarcastic, devastating, and Max listening, smiling, spurring him on. They would all three be altering and controlling the political world.

But for all three of them it was: once a real friend, always a real friend.

When after Ronald had been killed at Dunkirk I wrote his Biography, I asked Winston to do the Preface. He agreed immediately and in it he said:

Ronald Cartland was a man of noble spirit, who followed his convictions without thought of personal advancement. At a time when our political life had become feckless and dull, he spoke fearlessly for Britain. His words and acts were instinct with the sense of our country's traditions and duty. His courage and bearing inspired those who met him or heard him.

It was a very sincere token for he had loved Ronald, and during the retreat from Dunkirk, when no man could have been busier or more apprehensive of the future, he had taken the time to personally ring my mother three times in the country, to ask if there was any news of Ronald.

That is friendship, that is the love which is given from a full heart.

That is what Winston had, a heart boundless and with unplumbed depths for those he loved and whom he never forgot – as we shall never forget him.

Diana's wedding, June 1919.

The most beautiful woman in the world in *The Miracle*. Diana played the Madonna one night, the Nun the next.

When Diana left for America she wrote to Duff; "My heart seems to tear my body with pain for the loss of you."

LADY DIANA COOPER

She could only be born of love because she is so breathtakingly beautiful.

I have always believed and proved it many times, that if at the moment of conception, the fire of love evolves the life force ecstatically, then the child of such a union will be beautiful.

This contention is shown in history when love-children might have wild turbulent characters but they were certainly beautiful with positive personalities.

I first met Lady Diana Cooper and her husband on that never-to-be forgotten visit to Deauville in 1924.

Her photographs were familiar to everyone in the country but they could not portray her blue eyes – the colour of the Mediterranean very early in the morning when the rising sun touches the mists – her skin, white yet transparent like the perfection of eggshell porcelain, her hair, pale gold and with the delicate texture of ancient Chinese silk.

I had heard so many of the fantastic, exotic tales which had grown up round her during the war. She fell through a skylight watching fireworks in peace week 1919 and broke her leg; she was the first person I ever heard of to use black sheets; she played the lead in the first British film, and was one of the first women to own her own two-seater car in 1921.

I remember the reports of her marriage in 1919 when, as a reigning beauty and a Duke's daughter, she attracted the huge crowds which, in the years to come, would only turn out in such numbers for Royal processions and for film stars.

I had expected someone very far divorced from ordinary mortal interests – my expectations were quite incorrect.

To begin with, Lady Diana was as gay as a child as we started off down Southampton Water. She made us laugh, she banished the slight awkwardness which attends any party where half the company are strangers to each other.

But things were not to continue so smoothly. We ran into bad weather. The *Mairi* pitched and tossed – to my mind she seemed to be doing her best to stand on her head. I retired below.

My cabin-door was opened to bring the news that we had turned round and were going back to Southampton.

"Thank goodness! But why?"

"Diana has insisted. She thinks it is dangerous. She is always frightened at sea."

We crossed to Deauville by the ordinary cross-Channel steamer. The yacht went over without passengers; she took two days and only just made harbour. Everything on board that was movable was smashed. Two other yachts were wrecked in the storm.

I felt that Lady Diana had saved my life.

We reached Deauville, and the greatest beauty of the century arrived at the most dressed-up, bejewelled, money-conscious spot in the world without an evening-dress.

She and her husband were going on to New York where she had been engaged to play *The Miracle*. They were joining their ship at Cherbourg and all their luggage had already gone aboard.

"Someone will lend me a dress," Lady Diana said airily.

Two months later she was to give up her part as the Madonna and rush home to England at twelve hours' notice to help her husband win his seat at Oldham in the General Election.

She loved Duff overwhelmingly, protectively, adoringly. No two people could ever have been happier.

Some years later I saw Lady Diana in the cloakroom of the Embassy Club. I approached her shyly because she always seemed to me like a goddess far removed from mere mortals like myself.

"I must thank you, Lady Diana, for saving my life. If you hadn't turned the yacht round that time we were going to Deauville, I am certain it would have gone to the bottom and we should have all been drowned."

"I was glad to save my own life," she answered.

Her blue eyes were almost as translucent as the mirror which reflected them, her hair golden as pale corn, her face that of a saint.

I couldn't help being in awe of her, she was so beautiful, so regal. She gave me a smile that was almost a benediction, and with chiffon fluttering round her like angels' wings she went upstairs.

How was I to know that in the Second World War she would write:

> Yesterday I bought a seven-year-old cow for twenty-seven pounds. I milked her with speed and success. She gave over a gallon and a half and it only took me twenty minutes!

How could I guess? And how could I have imagined this:

> The Pig Family Hutchinson is in splendid fatness and should make me a nice profit . . . I spend a lot of time asphyxiated by the smell and bent double inside the sty, shovelling their dung.

When I think of Diana Cooper's beauty I know that only Maurice Baring put it in its proper perspective:

> Yet out of nothing God made time and space
> The stars, the sun, the summer and your face.

Lady Cunard.

The fantastic Mrs. Corrigan and some of her guests.

Lady Louis Mountbatten.

Lady Diana Cooper.

Lady Lettice Lyg

The Hon Mrs Richard Norton.

Lady Brownlow.

Lady Plunket.

MRS. LAURA CORRIGAN

Laura Corrigan managed by sheer willpower, vitality and money to gate-crash London Society.

A telephone operator in Cleveland, she had made a blind date with a steel millionaire who was drinking heavily and married him the following morning.

When he died six months later his wife inherited all his steel holdings. These she sold for $80,000,000 in cash. Laura Corrigan came to England and was presented at Court by the American Ambassadress in 1922.

On arriving in London she rented the house of Mrs. George Keppel (the last love of Edward VII) in Grosvenor Square, and asked for the owner's guest-list to be included in the lease. Mrs. Keppel agreed, but raised the rent.

Mrs. Corrigan started her sensational parties by asking anyone who would come, but in a few years only Royalty, smart Society and Press reporters could get in.

She introduced cabaret acts we had never seen before, acrobats, tap-dancers, and in the tombola were gold and diamond cigarette-cases, cuff-links and vanity cases.

In 1926 Mrs. Corrigan, inspired by the Bright Young People, made her guests provide the entertainment.

We couldn't have improved on the programme which was headed: "All Star Theatre, 16 Grosvenor Street, July 12th."

Guests were in fancy-dress for the dinner party which was just like any other, except that all the men were given silver pencils, and the women silver mirrors.

Afterwards the fun began. 'The Plantation Group' included Lady Louis Mountbatten – B. Natural (always am) – her cousin, the Countess of Brecknock, and Lord Ashley – B. Sharp (in business). There was a dancer – Beauty Nimble Legs. "This little darling," said the programme, "is the favourite of the Terpsichore" and was of course, Lady Plunket.

Mrs. Corrigan used to make innumerable 'malapropisms' which were sneered at and repeated with glee, especially by those who enjoyed her hospitality. Her first was to describe her house in Grosvenor Square as 'my little *ventre-à-terre*'. Another was when she said of a cathedral that it had 'magnificent flying buttocks'.

When Elsie de Wolfe, the decorator, who was also Lady Mendl, showed Mrs. Corrigan her villa at Versailles, she pointed out the indirect lighting which was new in those days.

"I just love this confused lighting," Laura Corrigan gushed.

I was never certain if she was really so naïve, or whether it was a very clever act.

Mrs. Corrigan always wore a wig owing to some accident in her early life which had left her completely bald. It was said she had a smart one which represented 'just come from the hairdresser', a dishevelled one 'just off to the hairdresser', and a windswept one.

One of Lady Cunard's more piquant remarks was when Laura Corrigan asked her what she was going to wear at the Opera that evening.

"Just my tiara and my own hair," Emerald replied.

As the years passed, Mrs. Corrigan got grander and grander. To get the people she wanted to her parties she sent the invitations out with co-hostesses who were too important for anyone to ignore. The card invariably bore the magic word 'decorations'.

Always a showman, she engaged experts to teach her and her friends the 'Big Apple' when it came in, and the 'Lambeth Walk'. Presents, like their recipients, got more and more impressive. Prince Frederick of Prussia and Dukes were presented with a pair of gold-mounted sock-suspenders! Lower titles received initialled braces with solid gold tabs, women were given gold and tortoise-shell combs in pink leather Cartier cases.

It was some years before Mrs. Corrigan's guests realised that the prize-winners were never commoners. Loelia Westminster (the 3rd Duchess) wrote:

> She worked through the Duchesses in strict order of precedence and shortly before the war she reached me. When I was handed the gold cigarette-case there were cat-calls and boos from my friends which Mrs. Corrigan took as a sign of my appalling unpopularity. It was beyond me to explain that what they objected to was the raffle being rigged.

In 1931 she rented the Palazzo Mocenigo in Venice where Byron had loved so romantically.

As Lady Diana Cooper put it: "She married the Adriatic and seemed to be holding the palaces in fee."

But she added: "Laura really has the world's happiness at heart."

She not only gave magnificent presents to her guests, she put notices in their bedrooms telling them not to tip the servants, never to buy cigarettes or stamps, not to pay for their washing or the drinks they had in the Grand Hotel and Lido Bar.

When the Germans overran France in 1940 she was living there, but refused to leave for America, like most of her countrymen, and remained in Paris.

Her stunt parties were over, she no longer stood on her head. Instead she sold her fabulous jewels one by one. The fat repulsive arms of Hermann Goering were covered from wrist to elbow under his uniform with bracelets he bought from the ex-telephone operator from Cleveland. She spent the proceeds in feeding French prisoners of war held by the Nazis.

Laura Corrigan had guts! That is why I have included her in this book.

The Earl and Countess close together in 1
at the marriage of their second daughter
Lady Dorothy to Sir Keith Frazer.
When the Earl died aged ninety-one in 193
the Countess after sixty-five years could n
live without him and died three days later.
They were buried together in the little chur
at Crome where they had always
worshipped, among the country people wh
loved them.

THE EARL AND COUNTESS OF COVENTRY'S DIAMOND WEDDING

On their Diamond Wedding Anniversary the Earl said of his wife: "She is the best wife a man ever had and a true helpmate."

Crome Hall, where the dear old couple live
and where there were marvellous parties
when I was a child, is now a Roman Catho
Home for mentally handicapped children

THE 9th EARL OF COVENTRY

When I was two years old my grandfather who was a financier lost all his money and we moved to a small house in Pershore in Worcestershire. Our landlord was the Earl of Coventry who was a kind friend to my father and mother all his life.

He was a marvellous old man, a great character and great gentleman.

He had been Captain and Gold Stick of the Corps of Gentlemen at Arms, Master of the Buckhounds, and when I knew him, was Lord Lieutenant of Worcestershire.

He used to tell me stories of his early life.

At the age of seven he had walked to church hand-in-hand with the great Duke of Wellington; he remembered going to lunch with Lord and Lady Palmerston; he had been staying at Tanby Croft, and recalled a famous occasion when one of the guests was caught cheating at cards. He had been called out of bed to advise the Prince of Wales, (later Edward VII) and the other guests on what to do.

'Covey', as he was always known, wore a low high hat, a 'bird's eye' tie of blue and white spots under his old-fashioned collar, a check waistcoat and cut-away coat.

He lived in great style at Crome Hall where I went to fabulous children's parties and once he said to my mother:

"I always judge a home and the people who own it by their servants."

He went on to explain that he believed that countries got the governments and people the servants they deserved.

At Newmarket in 1923 I saw Lord Coventry's horse Verdict beat the French horse, Epinaid in the Cambridgeshire by an 'eyelash'. The whole course cheered him and the King shook him by the hand saying:

"Coventry, I would far rather that you had won than that I had won myself!"

On the Earl's sixtieth wedding anniversary someone said to his wife who had produced thirteen children and hunted up to the day before each one was born:

"How delightful it must be for you and your husband to have been such close friends for sixty years."

"Friends? Friends?" the Countess questioned indignantly. "Covey and I have been lovers for sixty years and will be for many years more. Friends indeed!"

Noel was aged ten when he first appeared on the stage. He became the great genius of the theatre — the Master.

"If you gave people the chance," he said, "they would steal unscrupulously the heart and soul out of you without really meaning to."

Noel and I, both poor, unknown, insecure in 1921 at a party we hated Deauville. Then suddenly everyone was talking about *The Vortex*. Noe arrived!

NOEL COWARD

I met Noel first in 1924 at Deauville. We both hated the place and the party we were with.

I thought him bumptious and we quarrelled at luncheon until he called me 'Queen Gloom' and I burst into tears. After that he was sweet to me.

He took me to the 'chemmy' table, I sat beside him, he gave me money to play with and looked as pleased when I won as if he was listening to the applause he was to receive two months later when *The Vortex* took London by storm.

I never knew how truly it was 'the poor helping the poor' until I read Noel's own reminiscences. In his book *Present Indicative* he says that he then had only thirty pounds in the bank. I had only a few pounds to last me until the end of the month.

Noel also tells how while we were at Deauville Sir Jimmy Dunn offered to pay him twelve hundred pounds for five years on the understanding that he received twenty per cent of everything Noel earned during that period. After this offer had been made, Jimmy asked Noel to play to us. The only available piano was in the deserted dining room of the Royal Hotel. Noel writes:

> It was a strange setting: piled-up tables, shuttered windows, a dust-sheet pushed half off the piano and a few palms in pots looking, under the sharp electric light, as though they were going to be sick. I felt somehow that I was singing for my life.

I sat listening to Noel. The first hour I enjoyed myself. I loved his tunes, his songs. I remember *Parisian Pierrot* which Gertrude Lawrence had sung in *London Calling*, and *You Were Meant for Me*, the duet she and Noel had done together.

I had seen Noel's revue before I left London. I had been in a box with a party which included a rampageous young man who had been funny with a toy elephant. At the end of the show he had thrown it on the stage. I made no mention of this incident to Noel; I felt he was unlikely to think it amusing.

He played on and on. It was stuffy in the dining room and outside, for the first time since we had arrived in Deauville the rain ceased and a shamefaced sun made a feeble appearance. I wished Noel would stop! I wanted activity, movement and, indeed, fresh air.

When his performance ended there was just time to drop into the Casino before dinner!

Noel had however become a friend. That meant all through the years until he died he didn't change: he was always the same – kind, sympathetic, witty but never, to a friend , cruel.

When I wrote my biography of the Twenties *We Danced All Night*, Noel wrote to me:

> I have enjoyed every page which filled me with nostalgia. What a long time we have known each other! And how nice and satisfactory that is. My thanks and congratulations and my love, as always.
>
> Noel. xxx

To the world he was 'The Master', the cynic, the wit, the Englishman who lived abroad to save tax, but to his friends he gave his unchanging, unalterable love.

SIR JAMES DUNN

Lord Beaverbrook had three very great friends. They telephoned each other every day. Then consulted each other on every possible subject, and they appeared to me to be like four dashing Adventurers.

They were ambitious, determined, objective, riding rough-shod over those who got in their way, but having the grace, the charm and the irresistible flamboyance of their seventeenth-century counterparts.

Besides Lord Birkenhead and Sir Winston Churchill the third Adventurer was Sir James Dunn.

He was a Canadian like Max, a man of great wealth. When he died, he left twenty-five million!

He was a financier, and had been knighted during the war. He was rough and bluff, dominant and domineering.

He was the least polished of the four Cavaliers and the least self-controlled.

He would rage at the servants, be excessively rude in restaurants, and yet when he wished, he could exercise a charm that matched his blue eyes and the blue shirts he always wore.

Jimmy Dunn, who was in the process of having a divorce and had a grown-up family, asked me to marry him.

My mother was appalled, but I had no intention of marrying a man who I felt at fifty-four, was old enough to be my grandfather.

I was, however, fascinated by the life Jimmy lived which was more spectacular and more glittering than that of any of his friends.

Jimmy had rented an enormous house in Roehampton, not far from 'The Vineyards' called 'Templeton'.

It had a huge garden in which he gave floodlit parties to entertain an amazing variety of people.

There were Statesmen, politicians and actresses, film stars, millionaires and the 'Bright Young People'. We were entertained by Russian orchestras and singers, bands and ballerinas.

Like a character in a Wild West film, Jimmy, virile, forceful and overpowering, dominated every party, surrounding himself with all the trappings of the luxurious ultra-rich.

There was a fleet of Hispano Suizas to carry one from place to place, whole floors of hotels booked anywhere he wished to stay, and naturally a chorus of lovely women to amuse him whenever he wished to be amused.

introduced Jimmy
o his second wife,
he Marchioness of
Queensbury, and he
an away with her.

Jimmy's third wife Christofor — the only woman who could manage him and make him really happy. Now a successful racehorse owner.

Jimmy as Caesar for the frontispiece of *Courage*, his story written by his greatest friend Lord Beaverbrook. Tempestuous, unpredictable, but brilliantly clever with a charm he could turn on and off like a tap. He made a huge fortune and had three wives.

His mistress, a beautiful cultured woman, kept his interest for many years because she knew he liked weak, helpless women.

Whenever Jimmy appeared to be getting bored with her she had a surgical operation. He was whole-heartedly devoted to her until she was well again.

He asked me to go with a party to Deauville, then the most fashionable resort in France. When I agreed, taking with me as a chaperone the young and lovely Marchioness of Queensbury, we travelled in Lord Birkenhead's yacht and after an adventurous crossing of the Channel found that Jimmy had booked as usual a whole floor of the largest hotel in Deauville, and a party of over twenty were waiting for us.

I disliked Deauville because I was too young for the sophistication of it. I didn't understand what was happening, I was bored with the endless rich meals at which everyone drank too much while I didn't drink alcohol.

And Jimmy, true to form, behaved like a rough sea, with squawls, tempests, sudden bursts of sunshine, but never a dead calm.

Finally, after a week of incredible luxury and incessant gambling, Jimmy ran away with my friend, the Marchioness of Queensbury!

They were married after various vicissitudes, but he only found happiness with his third and last wife. He was a strange man, a very vital one, with an amazing brain, a capacity for friendship which made him exceedingly kind to me until his dying day, while at the same time, being nerve-rackingly unpredictable.

Looking back, I think he wanted to change the world round him by fighting it with both fists flying.

He was really born too late, he should have been blazing a trail over the Prairies in the days when a man with his vitality could, by leadership and determination, win against incredible odds.

I shall always be glad to have known him.

General Eisenhower inspected a Guard of Honour provided by the Black Watch when they were stationed in Berlin.

Ike's wife Mamie was pretty, had dar hair with 'bangs' and a nice voice.

Ike acknowledging the crowds on his way to St. Paul's with Prime Minister Harold MacMillan.

GENERAL DWIGHT EISENHOWER

My husband and I were determined as soon as the war ended to get our sons to a good day-school in London, so we rented a very attractive house called Hays Lodge in Chesterfield Hill in Mayfair, only to receive a set-back when the 'doodle' bombing started.

We, therefore, had to remain in Bedfordshire where we had been since 1940. I was rung up on the telephone one day and asked if I would rent Hays Lodge to a '*very, very important person*'.

I was told the whole arrangement was so hush-hush that I could not be told the name of the tenant, but I knew he was American, and when an enormous General's sword arrived before the rest of his luggage, it was not hard to guess who he was.

The appointment of General Dwight Eisenhower as Allied Commander was a very imaginative act on the part of President Roosevelt. The General had, I was told, never seen a shot fired in anger, and very little military experience, but he had a rare genius for smoothly co-ordinating the activities of an inter-allied staff.

It was later I was told that General Eisenhower learnt he was to be Supreme Commander of the Allied Invasion Forces from President Roosevelt when they were both staying at Carthage.

The President, his long cigarette-holder between his fingers, merely said:

"Well, Ike, you'd better begin packing your duds. You're going to London."

There was a considerable fuss before this when my decorator who was getting the house ready, asked me to provide linen. This I refused to do, as linen was now unobtainable in England except on coupons.

"But you *must*," she insisted. "No one can do too much for this splendid man."

I still refused, but my great friend who was the wife of the Queen's brother, the Hon. Michael Bowes-Lyon, lent a lot of her linen. Unfortunately, a boon to souvenir hunters, it all was embroidered with the Bowes-Lyon family crest.

After General Eisenhower had left Hays Lodge there was not one towel, sheet or pillow-case to be found!

When I met him I felt his vibrations were those of one who was sensitively attuned to everyone to whom he spoke.

He had a way of looking deep into the eyes of the person he was talking to, as if he searched beneath the surface for the truth.

He had a delightful, all-enveloping smile which forced one to smile back, and a sense of humour.

The war diary of Captain Harry Butcher, U.S.N.R., who was the Naval Aide to General Eisenhower, reports:

> When we reached London on 14 January England was wrapped in fog. An attractive house called Hays Lodge, Chesterfield Hill, had been furnished for Ike . . . When Ike was away we had two sharp bomb raids. A 1000-kilo bomb hit St. James's Square . . .
>
> I have reconnoitred the neighbourhood around Hays Lodge to find an appropriate shelter into which Ike might be introduced and have found one . . . It is an old wine cellar of a house built by Lord Clive and has bed, blankets, electric heaters and a kitchen.
>
> It is operated by the Oxford Group and was built before the War, but probably after the Oxford Group had decided that Hitler was not one of their adherents. Ike merely mentioned that it seemed to him a bit incongrous for him as a military leader to seek safety in an air-raid shelter run by pacifists!

In Hays Lodge special telephones were installed beside the flame-coloured velvet bed in my bedroom. The Nile-blue walls had been matched from a scarab I had been given in Luxor many years earlier.

In my green drawing room and pine-panelled dining room many important decisions were made. The dining room was built out at the back and as the light came from a skylight it was certainly a vulnerable target.

Edwina Mountbatten told me how one night when she dined there with General Eisenhower, the Prime Minister – Winston Churchill – General Sir Hastings Ismay, Chief of Staff, and other important people, bombs were falling outside and there were crashing repercussions.

Everyone at the table ignored the noise and the frequent vibrations, talking and laughing as if nothing was happening; but the General's black servants brought in the soup with unsteady hands and after the first course all appeared in tin hats!

The black servants, incidentally, slept in the only safe room in the house, which, being underground and reinforced, was known as 'the air-raid shelter'.

General Eisenhower was always very smart, and even in the heat of battle looked as if he had come straight out of a band-box.

The servants' sitting room at Hays Lodge was turned into a 'tailor's shop' – at least that's what the Americans called it; and when they said the General would want the room for his 'tailor', I could not think what they meant until I discovered that the tailor was what we call a valet.

After the war when, as always happens, the cheers turn to criticism and the inevitable debunking starts over any great leader, all sorts of different aspects of General Eisenhower's character were presented to the public.

But perhaps one very human story of the great man is worth recording. Soon after he moved into Hays Lodge, I was rung up by one of his Aides-de-Camp to ask if I would permit them to remove the struts on the dining room table.

As this was a very valuable, very old oak refectory table with beautifully carved legs I was horrified.

"Of course you can't cut it about," I said firmly, "the struts have been there for four hundred years and you will ruin the table if you try to remove them."

"If we don't the old man will kick them to pieces!" his Aide replied.

They were removed!

Beautiful, brilliant, exotic Maxine captivated every man she met.

The glamorous Château de l'Horizon, where Maxine swam and grew fat.

MAXINE ELLIOTT

As I entered the hall of the Château de l'Horizon at Cannes I saw a picture of a beautiful woman, dark, glorious, imperious, hanging on the stairs.

"Is that Maxine Elliott?" I asked.

"Everyone asks that," was the reply. "It is exactly as she looked thirty years ago, but it was in fact, painted in the sixteenth century."

"How extraordinary!" I exclaimed.

"Maxine's mother had it hanging at the end of her bed and she looked at it all the time the child was on the way. Maxine grew up to be so like it, that it was uncanny!"

Maxine Elliott, whose sister had married the famous actor-manager, Sir John Forbes-Robertson, had been a legend for many years.

Beautiful, intelligent, talented, successful, she was the most glamorous actress on the American stage before the First World War.

She and Ethel Barrymore are the only actresses who have ever had a Broadway Theatre named after them.

Maxine came from a small town in Maine, and after she became enormously wealthy from her earnings and her friendship with H.P. Morgan, she resented the prejudice she encountered in America and came to England.

Her partner in the Maxine Elliott Theatre did everything he could to prevent her from retiring.

"You'll miss the glamour and glory of the stage," he predicted.

"I'll miss it as much as the Christian martyrs missed the man-eating lions in the arena!" she retorted.

After Maxine's retirement and she had made sure of King Edward's friendship, she decided to buy a house.

She found when she first arrived in England she was not invited to dinner parties by the hostesses who usually entertained the King. She therefore went to Marienbad with the sole purpose of getting to know him.

One morning when the King was on his way to the Kurkhaus with three friends, he became aware of a beautiful, spectacularly dressed woman sitting on a bench reading a book.

As His Majesty passed she raised her huge dark liquid eyes and they looked at each other. The Royal party went on but a little later one of the King's attendants returned:

"His Majesty believes you are Miss Elliott whom he admired so much in your play. His Majesty would be delighted with your presence tonight at the dinner Mrs. Arthur James is giving in His Majesty's honour at the Weimir Hotel. Your invitation will, of course, be delivered to you later."

Maxine, dressed in her smartest gown, waited for the invitation. It did not arrive. An hour passed, when the King must have arrived at Mrs. James's suite, and Maxine still waited. Inside the suite the new-fashioned cocktails were passed round. The butler bowed to the King.

"Will Your Majesty lead the guests in to dinner?"

"I am waiting for Miss Elliott," he replied.

A footman dashed to Maxine's apartments with a large white envelope.

Mrs. James tried to explain that the invitation for Miss Elliott must have dropped behind her desk.

Without hurrying Maxine accepted the card. When she arrived she did not show that she was aware that Mrs. James had attempted to defy the King by diplomatically forgetting the invitation.

His Majesty insisted the dinner should wait while Maxine drank her cocktail. For twenty minutes the whole party stood as the King did not sit down.

"How could you wait for so long?" Maxine's nieces asked her years later.

"I wanted to be there," Maxine repeated simply.

At a further visit to Marienbad the next year Maxine was seen frequently in the King's company. She then bought Hartsbourne Manor in Hertfordshire, and spent a great deal of money on the rooms above her own which were known as 'the King's Suite'!

She also entertained all the brilliant men of the period: Lord Birkenhead, Lord Kitchener, Lord Balfour, Winston Churchill, and after her divorce from an actor who had married eight times, the Marquess Curzon of Kedleston asked her to be his wife.

She became obsessed with bridge and backgammon and built herself a sound-proof room with the walls covered in black moiré silk.

Here she would play for hours undisturbed.

Maxine was generous with her money and paid for another famous actress – Constance Collier – to be treated for diabetes in Switzerland. She was one of the first patients to be cured by insulin.

When Maxine was forty-two she fell in love with Anthony Wilding, a New Zealand tennis champion aged twenty-seven. He was an exceptionally fine man. He loved Maxine with all his heart and she loved him.

On 4 August 1914, he was in the U.S.A. playing in the Davis Cup. He sailed the same night for England to join the Army.

She followed him across the Channel organising and paying for the expenses of the Canadian barges which moved along the canals of Belgium. In a year she fed and clothed approximately three hundred and fifty thousand refugees behind the Front Line.

In 1915 in the second battle of Ypres, Captain Tony Wilding was killed – with his death the light went out of Maxine's eyes and both her heart and her youth died with him.

She continued to devote all her energy to the Allied cause.

When the King of the Belgians, Albert I, presented Maxine with his country's highest civilian decoration, in pinning the medal on her dress, he pierced her breast.

"You have been wounded!" he exclaimed when he saw the blood seeping through the silk.

"Yes, Sir," she responded, "but not by the enemy!"

After the war Maxine built the Château de l'Horizon which I had been told before I went there was the most magnificent villa on the whole of the Côte d'Azur.

I expected Maxine to be unusual, but I had not thought I should find that now she was old she had grown enormously fat. She spent her days swimming in her enormous swimming-pool looking like a captive whale or sitting beside it playing backgammon.

It was still possible to visualise how beautiful she had been, for her huge dark eyes were unchanged and when she talked she was so fascinating that one was entranced by everything she had to say.

What I hated however, was Maxine's last and only love, a bad-tempered, smelly little monkey called Kiki. He made messes all over the beautiful villa, bit anyone who tried to touch him, and had a terrifying trick of springing unexpectedly on one's shoulder.

I found it difficult to concentrate on anything except on keeping away from Kiki. I hate monkeys, having once been shut up in the Monkey House at the Zoo with over a hundred of them.

We talked until luncheon was announced and sat down with a very large party. It was an enormous meal, and every dish had thick rich cream sauces.

I noticed that Maxine, despite her bulk, ate ravenously.

"I have just received my death sentence," she remarked to someone sitting next to her, "the doctor says I have uraemia. He says I must cut out all rich food."

She beckoned the butler to bring her another helping.

"You will kill yourself, Maxine, if you don't listen to him!" her friend cried.

"There's only one better way to die, and I'm too old for that!" she answered.

Arthur Elvin's swift climb to fame and fortune started at the Great British Exhibition at Wembley in 1924. I remember the Prince of Wales modelled in Canadian butter, and King George V on the scenic railway, grimly holding on to his bowler hat.

Arthur and his wife Jean at home.

Arthur with London's Lord Mayor Sir Bracewell Smith at Wembley which as a sporting centre had become fashionable. Although the Press made fun of the original Exhibition 27,000,000 people enjoyed the Rodeo, the reproduction of the Niagara Falls, the Tibetan musicians and the Dodgems.

SIR ARTHUR ELVIN

During the Great Wembley Exhibition in 1924, Jean, an attractive girl, was put in charge of the Ciro Pearls stand. On the next stand, which exhibited tobacco, there was a red-haired, large-nosed young man called Arthur Elvin.

Jean had little time for Arthur as she had been promised twenty pounds if she could persuade Queen Mary, who was a constant visitor to Wembley, to stop and look at the pearls.

Queen Mary obliged and inspected the pearls, and no sooner had she left than Arthur popped in to congratulate Jean. He suggested they should open a bottle of champagne.

"Thank you, Ginger, I can pay for my own drinks," Jean answered crushingly.

Arthur disliked being called 'Ginger' but he persevered.

"What about a little drink in the West End?"

"No," Jean replied, "not until you learn to dress properly."

Arthur was astonished; he usually wore very natty suits in green or mustard colour.

"What's wrong with my suit?" he demanded.

"Try blue!" Jean suggested, turning her back.

Arthur did try blue. The following year he assisted in the demolition of the Exhibition. He bought one small building, sold it at a profit and bought another. He re-sold the sites and later paid Jimmy White £122,000 for the Stadium, which he sold the same day for £150,000.

For a year or two the whole property hung fire. Then owing to Arthur Elvin's enterprise there came a resurrected Wembley, the new home of greyhound racing and international sport.

Nearly £90,000 was spent on the greyhound track; there was a car-park for four thousand vehicles and covered seating for thirty thousand spectators.

I was one of the original privileged guests to sample the restaurant, where one could bet, watch and eat. There was also a dance-floor. 'Going to the dogs' became smart as well as being a national pastime.

Arthur Elvin over the years was responsible for football cup-finals, speedway and car racing, horse shows, indoor lawn-tennis tournaments, swimming and ice-skating championships, basketball, hockey, water carnivals, ice pantomimes and a magnificent torchlight tattoo – the forerunner of those presented later at Aldershot.

I had a house at the seaside one summer and it was next door to the one owned by the Elvins. Jean, who adored Arthur, was very jealous and she would ask me again and again:

"What do you think Arthur is doing now?"

If she found out, she was prepared to go in with her fists and her handbag flying to claim her own!

Arthur was really a very ugly man, but he had that inexhaustible vitality and drive which had made him a success and of course women were attracted to him and he to them.

The two are synonymous.

DOUGLAS FAIRBANKS

The personification of charm, it is difficult to assess how astute Douglas Fairbanks is behind the handsome looks, the beguiling smile, the twinkling eyes and the slim, elegant figure which has cast him as the hero in hundreds of plays and films.

Like a woman with a pretty face whom no one expects to have brains as well, Douglas is too attractive for most people to look further than the famous smile.

But he has had great success in industry; his public service in the United States and internationally leaves one gasping. While among his numerous war activities, he headed and was personally responsible for the Douglas Voluntary Hospitals in the United Kingdom, he helped organise the Franco-British War Relief Inc., and The Fight for Freedom Committee.

His Honours, Awards, Orders, and Decorations fill eight pages of his biography and include the Silver Star Medal and Legion of Merit Medal for Valour from his own country, he won our Distinguished Service Cross and is a Knight Commander of the British Empire. He was awarded the Croix de Guerre with Palm by France.

Greece, Italy, Netherlands, Belgium, Chile, Brazil and Korea have all decorated him.

But what is the real Douglas Fairbanks like behind the smile?

He had an unhappy childhood, overshadowed by his father, the swashbuckling film star hero, and he has worked desperately hard all his life to establish himself as himself.

He was, I think, from an early age, aware that he was Prince Charming without the stability of a throne and he had no wish to live in the reflection of his father's.

But with Douglas Fairbanks Senior and Mary Pickford, the world's sweetheart, as an example, what could he do but act? He was fourteen when he appeared in his first film in 1923 and seventeen in his first play. But he has written poems and short stories, personality profiles, essays, and articles, and exhibited his drawings, paintings and sculpture in Paris and the U.S.A.

It was President Roosevelt with his uncanny instinct for choosing the right man, who sensed that Douglas was a born diplomat and gave him official and unofficial duties in philanthropic and educational organisations and during the war appointed him as a Presidential Envoy on

A very rare photograph of Douglas with his mother.

Douglas with his wife Mary Lee and a few of his many medals.

The two best-looking and most fascinating men in the world, Lord Mountbatten and Douglas.

Douglas handsome, dashing and irresistible, *The Prisoner of Zenda*, one of the first grea heart-throbs.

Special Missions. But he served with the Navy from 1941–1946 and became a full Commander.

He has six decorations for combat, eleven for Diplomatic services, seven medals for Military campaigns, six Civilian and eight Honorary Degrees and Fellowships.

This fantastic record still leaves one looking for the real person behind the glitter.

I think that brought up in the unreal, cardboard world of Hollywood, where everything was pretence, nothing had any substance, Douglas has, all his life, wanted to be an ordinary normal man among ordinary normal people.

And because he used charm rather than prestige, because he was never puffed up with his consequence, because he was prepared to listen and to understand, he has been liked and trusted by everyone and every nation with whom he came into contact.

But because he had been quite humble to himself about himself, others have not realised how extraordinary he is.

In fact, he is a truly underestimated personality.

It would be tragic if to many people and perhaps to history, he is to be remembered only as a very handsome actor with an irresistibly charming smile.

Boris and Gracie.

Boris was a rock to Gracie's rolling sea, steadfast, wise, calm and very much in love with his scintillating wife.

GRACIE FIELDS

My son Glen and I went to Capri on the hydrofoil from Naples.

Capri with its flowers and misty mountains, its sunshine and its history of the Greek gods was breathtaking. I saw a good-looking man in a very smart grey suit standing by the swimming-pool. I felt sure it was Boris Alperovici, and I introduced myself. He said Gracie would love to see me.

We climbed steps which went straight up a precipice. I was 'panting and blowing' when we reached the top. Boris was quite unperturbed, he told me he did the climb dozens of times a day.

Gracie was just 'Gracie', her vivid personality filled her pretty sunlit sitting room and vibrated like the waves below. She was unmistakably and brilliantly a star. She glittered, and I could only gasp in admiration. We 'covered the world' in a short scintillating conversation!

She looked very much the same as she had the first time I met her in 1930. We had both been on the stage of the London Pavilion with the Prince of Wales for a fantastic Midnight Matinee, which raised £12,000 for charity.

When we left Boris took us through a flower-filled garden to their gate where our car was waiting. He was absolutely delightful. I could understand only too well what Gracie meant when she wrote:

> All the love stories I'd ever read, all the sentimental songs I'd ever sung, I really understood now for the first time in my life.

I thought of Gracie Fields starting work in a mill and becoming one of the most loved personalities of our time.

When I read her life story, *Sing As We Go*, I understood that the reason she touched everyone's heart was because she wanted to share herself with us. She explains her feelings, when at the Coliseum Boris for the first time sees her perform in a London Theatre:

> I felt as though a hundred champagne corks had popped inside my heart. I wanted to make the whole world laugh and be happy with me. My voice wasn't enough for once. In the middle of the show the whole bubbling loveliness that was life for me just burst and I turned a cartwheel! I had to do something!

I saw Gracie turn that cartwheel and I now understood why everyone in that huge theatre cheered and clapped her with tears running down their cheeks.

When I got home I sent Gracie my book on *Josephine Empress of France*. She wrote me a postcard saying:

> Thank you so much. I had a wonderful time with Josephine, enjoying every word. The first time I ever got to know the lady; most, most interesting had to keep reading it aloud to Boris who enjoyed it with me. Bless you, and once again thank you . . . Gracie.

Her warmth and her love came from the very paper on which she had written in her large, clear handwriting.

ROSITA FORBES

Rosita Forbes was the first woman explorer in the early Twenties, to set off alone to see the remote and dangerous parts of North Africa and the Near East.

She visited Kufara, the secret city of the Sahara, and Jizan in Asir, where no white woman had ever been before. Disguised as a Bedouin woman she even tried to get through to Mecca.

"Were you frightened?" I asked, knowing that had she been discovered it could have meant instant death.

"No! Only footsore," she replied, showing me her feet.

They were cut, bruised, calloused, the heels rough and blistered from walking barefoot. In 1925 a film, *From Red Sea to Blue Nile*, was made from Rosita's stories of her travels.

She was very resourceful. She told me that once having travelled for miles across a desert, she arrived in some big town to find an invitation from Government House to dine at eight o'clock. The camel, or whatever had brought her there, had been slower than usual, and she found she only had a few minutes in which to dress.

She pulled open her bag with her lace evening-dress in it, and then discovered to her consternation, that she had forgotten to pack her stockings. Of course they had to be black – there were only black or dead white stockings in those days – and anyway Rosita's dress was of black lace.

"I had my evening shoes," she said, "but there was no time to buy stockings and as I had never been to this Government House before, I knew no one from whom I could borrow a pair. Besides, there just wasn't time. It would have been unthinkable to keep their Excellencies waiting."

"What did you do?" I asked.

"Luckily there was a coal fire in my bedroom which had not been lit," she said. "I blacked my legs with coal dust. I thought it smelt a little peculiar, so I covered myself with scent and swept downstairs. Nobody noticed, and although I say it myself, I was a success that evening."

There was no one as daring as Rosita and she didn't look at all like an intrepid explorer. She was tall, slender, and fragile-looking, very attractive to men with an oval face and large protruding eyes.

Needless to say not everyone admired her daring. People were extremely shocked at the idea of a woman going off 'into the blue' on

At my Railway Train Ball.

Exploring.

Rosita aged twenty-

her own. It was 'unfeminine'. But Rosita was seeking something indefinable, as we all were.

The Queen of Egypt, strictly secluded, asked her:

"Why did you want to go to Kufara?"

Rosita said afterwards:

"How could I explain? It was certainly not for ambition, I travelled – like Elroy Flecker's Merchants in Hassan – for lust of knowledge and in answer to a deep aching need to learn more about the desert and its life."

The French Geographical Society gave Rosita their gold medal. The only other woman previously to be accorded this honour was Mme. Curie, the discoverer of radium.

Rosita was poised, calm and controlled whether she was in danger of being denounced as a spy or facing death from a Berber knife.

In a pageant that I arranged for the Train Ball at Covent Garden, I asked Rosita to come as 'The Royal Highlander'. She had fifty yards of red velvet train to manipulate – a difficult experience for anyone – but Rosita managed it with the same efficiency as she must have used to control a grumpy camel.

She had before the Second World War a very lovely house in London, but it was one of those destroyed by the Germans, and she decided to leave England and build herself a home on Eleuthera Island, near Nassau.

She began by living in a tent, something she was quite used to, while she watched her house being built brick by brick. She wrote to me:

> The hardest part is cutting a way through a wilderness of thicket.

That was what she had been doing all her life – not only a natural wilderness, but a wilderness of prejudice against women being explorers, unveiled and unsecluded.

She was, although she had no idea of it, a pioneer of Women's Lib.

Her magnetic personality radiates from her wherever she goes.

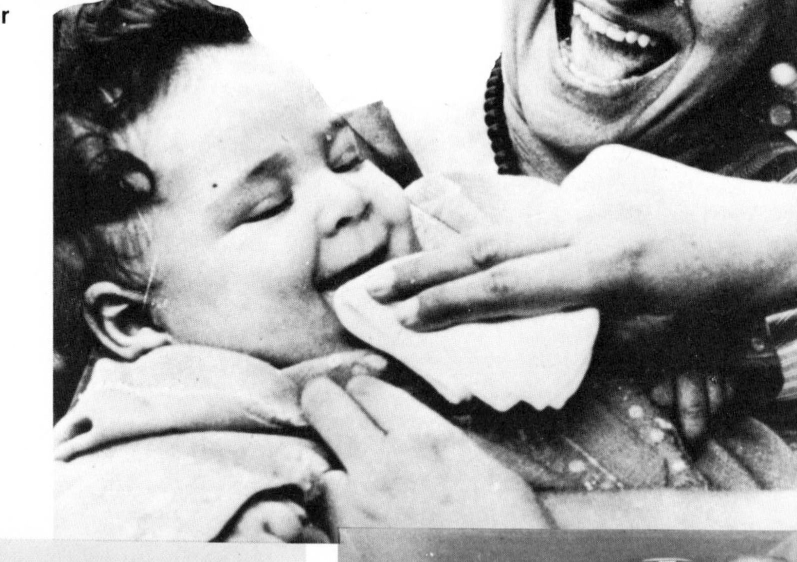

The woman who rules over 600 million people with one of her grandchildren. She loves them and they love her.

With her two sons. When Sanjay was killed flying, she was broken-hearted.

I took Mrs. Gandhi when she was out of office, to see Lord Mountbatten, the last Viceroy. They had a mutual admiration for each other.

INDIRA GANDHI

I met Indira first in 1959. Wearing a blue sari, she was slim, quiet and gentle. Although she was already holding one of the most important posts in Congress, she was overshadowed by the overwhelming personality of her father Pandit Nehru.

When he died in 1964, one of the really great men of the century, Indira wrote to me:

> A great void has been left in the lives not only of those who were privileged to be close to him, but of so many others who did not even know him. We are fortunate in having so many happy memories of him, and these must help to comfort us all in our grief.

I knew that she was grateful for the years of love and inspiration of someone she adored.

Two years later aged fifty-eight, Indira became Prime Minister of India. It seemed fantastic that with all the talk of emancipation and equality for women in Britain and America the East should give a second woman the greatest political position in her country.

From that moment I have watched Indira develop and become a magnificently outstanding character, if a controversial one.

The problems and difficulties she has faced, the opposition and aggressive treatment even from her own people, have only strengthened her. Like all those in the East whose very being is deep-rooted in an indestructible faith, she is undefeatable and her courage shines through her like a light.

Like her father, Indira has grown in the public mind until one thinks of her as one of the 'big' people, and I am astonished every time I see her, how small in height she actually is.

But while I admire her whole-heartedly for what she has achieved for India – and that is a great deal – while her bravery in adversity makes me proud, I love her for her femininity and her sense of humour.

I have never forgotten on one visit, when the stress of strikes, food shortages and riots must have been almost intolerable, and I was told the Prime Minister was very tired and had been suffering from 'flu, she came hurrying into the room where I was waiting for her.

"I am so sorry, dear Barbara!" she exclaimed, "but I have not had time to change my sari, and I know you hate me in brown."

The tenderness in her eyes when she plays with her grandchildren, the way she keeps the coloured paper and the ribbons in which her gifts are wrapped to use again, her delight in a new face-cream, are very feminine too.

I adored her dry sense of humour when she was told she was to go to prison, and she remarked:

"It will be a nice rest!"

In a letter she wrote to me a little while ago she said:

You are beautiful outside, because you are beautiful inside.

That is the secret of her success – she always looks deeply beneath the surface. In my conversations with her I have been aware that she is not satisfied with what she has been told or what she has seen, she knows instinctively there is more to be discovered – perhaps to be exposed.

The esoteric, the spiritual, is so vital in the East, so easily recognisable, that the barriers between it and the physical are often indefinable.

That, I know, is the reason why one small woman has been able to rule 600 million people, and for the vast number of them to give her not only their allegiance but their hearts.

Indira's power comes from the ageless, unchanging, eternal force she transmits through herself. To the West it is incomprehensible, but to the East it is the only real way of life.

ELINOR GLYN

She influenced me from the time I was sixteen.

I did not know then of her outstanding beauty, of the swimming-bath her husband hired on their honeymoon so that she could swim naked with her flowing red hair trailing in the water, of her need for money so that to pay off debts she must write at a speed only beaten later by me, of the sensational scandal she evoked with *Three Weeks* which I was forbidden to read.

I was enthralled by *The Visits of Elizabeth*, a barely concealed biography of Elinor's own début into society.

Elizabeth describes herself:

> Timid, really and very tender-hearted – and always antagonistically treated by women for no reason except nature's bizzare choice of red, white and green – always the centre of the passionate love of men – always proud – always alone.

That, I felt, was me! Only my colouring was slightly different – *gold*, white and green!

The whole story was mine too! Elizabeth's innocence and the mistakes she made and the proposals of marriage she received were mine! When she captured her Marquis that too I felt would be my fate eventually.

By the time I met Elinor Glyn she was very much older and so was I, but I still found her exciting, romantic and very glamorous.

By then her most important lover, the Marquess Curzon of Kedleston, had married a rich woman and with incredible brutality had only let her know when she saw his engagement announced in *The Times*.

To her, he was as she had said in a letter to him:

> You are you, for me the sun, moon and stars and the end of time!

No one could have behaved with greater pride or more like the 'ladies' in her novels than Elinor. She burnt the five hundred letters he had written her and never mentioned his name again!

But love was her life and she was passionate until she died. She said to a young man – of course he had a title:

Elinor on a tiger skin. She was given two, one from Lord Curzon, one from Lord Milner.

Elinor looked radiantly beautiful at Court and made six curtseys faultlessly.

The Marquess Curzon of Kedleston — Elinor's dream lover.

"You shall be my last lover – I will teach you the divine ecstasy of absolute love as no one else could do."

She was astounded when he refused.

She visited Russia and read the novel she wrote about it to the Tsar and Tsarina; she found the mining camps of Nevada were a 'turning-point' in her spiritual progress. She toured the battlefields during the war.

She invented the word 'It' to describe the magnetic, what we would call now the sexual attraction of a man or a woman. She took America by storm, she found a new secret and a successful method of remaining young.

But her looks, wildly, dramatically, tempestuously romantic, all extolled the right principles, the dignity of those where were born ladies and gentlemen and the supreme sacrifice of self for the glory of love.

She had a fire, a buoyant energy, a creative urge, an iron self-control, and a will of steel.

She also definitely, unmistakably, compellingly had 'IT'!

Claude in front of the biplane in which he landed in street in America.

With his wife Ethel Levy. Singer and "hostess with the mostest" dark, seductive , very smart.

Dashing, romantic , at one time the world's gre aviator, it seems incredible that Claude is forgotten.

CLAUDE GRAHAM-WHITE

Claude Graham-White was the first Englishman to gain an aviator's certificate of proficiency. He was educated at Bedford, where he studied engineering, and when he learnt to fly he was one of Bleriot's first pupils. He owned the first petrol-driven motor-car in England and, having taken up flying in 1909, the following year he entered for flying races both in England and America, where he won the Globe Prize and Gordon Bennet Cup.

After this as England's favourite flyer he easily captured the cup for Royal Aero of Great Britian.

He also founded the first British flying school at Pau in France, and formed a company to run the Hendon Flying Club in London which he developed into the biggest British flying field of the day, and which was later sold for half a million pounds.

In 1910 when Claude Graham-White visited the United States State, War and Navy Departments, he landed his biplane on a street – West Executive Avenue, a main thoroughfare between the White House and the State, War and Navy Buildings.

He wrote many treatises on aircraft, its technical development and its use in war. He was commissioned in the Royal Naval Air Service in 1914 and took part in the first air-raid on German-held bases in Belgium.

Claude, who was tall, dark, thick-set and dashing, had a charm which women found irresistible.

When I knew him he was married to Ethel Levey, an American artiste with an aquiline nose. I had first seen her in 1914 in *Hello Ragtime*, which my father had taken me to just before war broke out.

In that show Ethel sang – in a deep, husky, passionate bass voice – with a sense of rhythm which has never been surpassed, even by Negroes.

Ethel was always called 'The Woman Who Fed Mayfair'. She was the first American before the war to entertain with the lavishness which was echoed later by Mrs. Corrigan. It was said that several Americans went broke trying 'to out-Ethel Ethel', and, of course, a great many people disliked her.

Ethel inaugurated many new fashions, including costume jewellery. Her 'trademark' was a large slave bangle round her ankle, and I never saw her without half a dozen golden bracelets hung with coins and charms. These were copied by women all over the world.

She and Claude were very much in love when I knew them and they both had a flamboyance which I found fascinating. Claude could not help flirting with every woman he met, young or old! He was magnetic, theatrical, and very sure of himself.

Claude had been married to another American before Ethel. She was Dorothy Taylor, who had inherited $15,000,000 from her father's leather business. After their marriage had only lasted three years, Dorothy became the Countess di Frasso, and her witty tongue and wild escapades made her adored by the gossip-writers of Europe until her death.

Dorothy had Claude and Ethel (who was her greatest friend) watched by a detective. She then dined out for weeks on the information that Ethel's bedroom ceiling was painted sky-blue with a picture of an aeroplane coming through the clouds, as if preparing for a forced landing on the bed!

"I married England's greatest aviator," Dorothy said once, "and then the greatest gentleman in Europe. It's a toss-up which jerk took me for more dough."

Claude died a rich man three days before his eightieth birthday. He had been fêted and acclaimed as Britain's first and most popular aviator. He had been one of the foremost pioneers to conquer the air.

His enthusiasm, his opportunism and his courage lives on but he, himself, has been forgotten.

THE HON. MRS. RONALD GREVILLE

The daughter of a Scottish brewer who was a Liberal Member of Parliament, a Privy Councillor and a millionaire, Mrs. Greville was socially impregnable, almost omnipotent.

She adored Royalty. Queen Mary often visited Polesden Lacey, her country home with a gold drawing room near Dorking, and other guests were the Duke and Duchess of York, who spent their honeymoon there, foreign Royalty, Ambassadors and eminent politicians.

She was powerful and knew it. She had strong likes and dislikes and as she was a shrewd judge of character she was usually right.

I met Mrs. Greville at Baden-Baden, and although I was introduced to her by a Viscount I was astonished when she invited me to drive with her in her large Rolls-Royce.

At the time I was trying to make a living by writing and had no close contact with the exalted circles in which Mrs. Greville spun her webs like a spider.

Enormous, ugly – Harold Nicolson described her as 'a fat slug filled with venom' – draped in magnificent gems and fantastic jewels, she drove me through the loveliest scenery in Europe while in a soft, secretive voice she poured out a stream of indiscretions.

She had a scandalous story to tell about everyone of importance, all of whom were her 'friends'.

Only Royalty was sacred – 'They are just like my own family.' Hitler had some protection as he was a Head of State. 'My dear little brown-shirts' were spoken of with affection.

Maggie Greville was clever enough to know that she could not attract people only by her enormous riches, she had to be interesting as well, and what was more interesting than indiscreet innuendos about everyone else?

The way she told them, in what from any other woman would have been a seductive voice, made them funnier and more insidious than they actually were.

She was in the centre of many different worlds, and used her power politically as well as socially.

I mentioned to her that my brother admired Lord Lloyd and she snorted before she replied:

"That dreadful man had the impudence to think he might be Viceroy of India, but I soon put a stop to that!"

A House Party at Polesden Lacey in 1909 with King Edward VII, the guest of honour.

Queen Mary wearing her fantastic pearls.

Polesden Lacey, now the property of the National Trust.

I learnt that Maggie Greville was generous, but she insisted on remaining anonymous when she gave some of her millions to charity.

"I've no wish to be like Lord—" she declared, "who blows a trumpet every time he puts a shilling in the collection-bag."

I laughed. I had heard that she often raised the hopes of those who made a practice of begging, then at the last moment slammed the door in their faces.

She was fantastic, dominating and overwhelming. It was like seeing a witch-ball swing round and round, and being mesmerised by it.

I admired her jewellery and she told me when she died it would all go to the Royal Family. I knew it gave her great satisfaction to think the huge pearls she had round her thick neck would keep such exalted company.

Then, on about our fourth meeting she mentioned the name of a man – of course titled – whom I knew.

"He is clever, I hear, and he hopes . . ."

"I had a letter from him yesterday," I interrupted quickly to prevent any uncomfortable revelation.

"You know him?" she asked in surprise.

"Yes, very well."

There was a pause.

"Is he in love with you?"

"He says so," I answered lightly.

There was a long silence.

"Men only want a pretty face!"

The sharpness in her voice was very revealing.

She was jealous!

"The happiest recollections would always be the early struggles, when every post was a winning post and every day brought new hope and fresh achievement."

With his daughter Barbara and her husband Nicholas Bentley.

A great advocate, a loyal friend, a loving husband and father, optimistic playwright, with an unquenchable joy of living.

SIR PATRICK HASTINGS, K.C.

'The greatest advocate at the Bar' was how Sir Patrick Hastings was described in the Twenties. He was so brilliantly perceptive in his presentation of a case that his wife said that when he knew the Jury was with him, he would often sit down without finishing his address or the sentence he was speaking.

Charming, artistic, original, amusing – there was more laughter and fun in the Hastings household than in any I have ever known. And their happiness lay in being all together.

Mary Hastings once told me that her husband had never accepted an invitation for them to stay away all the years they had been married. He could not bear to leave the children.

Sir Patrick lived a life of adventure. He had worked as a mining engineer in a Welsh goldfield, spent six months in a lightship, been a journalist, served in the Army during the South African War, been a dramatic critic, and was called to the Bar in 1904.

He would also have made a brilliant actor, but he satisfied that side of his diverse character by writing several successful plays.

He told me the story of how during the Boer War he was always up in front of a military tribunal on account of some crime he had committed.

On the last occasion he was also deeply worried by what he should do when the war ended. The Sergeant-Major who had arrested him somewhat incoherently endeavoured to describe his offences.

Angered by the eloquent way Pat defended himself, he remarked on leaving the Court:

"Hastings, you ought to be a bloody lawyer."

Pat was overcome with gratitude.

"You are quite right Sergeant-Major," he replied, "I shall!"

His wife, who had the loveliest expression it is possible to find on any woman's face – a very different thing to just being born with lovely features – ran away from home to marry Sir Patrick when he was an unknown barrister. They were very much in love and very, very poor.

Life became such a struggle that after Barbara, their eldest child, was born they decided to wait one more week, then if a brief wasn't forthcoming, they would pack up and go to New Zealand. The evening before the week expired a brief arrived!

Sir Patrick, the most generous, warm-hearted and kindly of men, could be – on social occasions which he loathed – both gruff and difficult. He wouldn't have admitted it but it was because he was shy. He hated his own weakness.

It made him an ardent Socialist, it made him aggressive and he would deliberately use bad language so that he sounded tough.

When out of the generosity of his warm heart he took my divorce case for nothing and of course won, as soon as I tried to thank him he said to my brother Ronald:

"This bloody case of your sister's has cost me a bloody two thousand pounds!"

In 1930 Ronald and I went to see Noel Coward's magnificent, but tear-jerking spectacular *Cavalcade* at Drury Lane.

We waved to Sir Patrick and his family in the theatre and afterwards we ran into them having supper at the Savoy Grill. Ronald asked Sir Patrick how he had enjoyed the show.

"Awful – worst thing I've ever seen!" he snapped.

His daughter Barbara laughed.

"Don't believe a word Daddy says. Why, he wept through every act!"

HIS EXCELLENCY TIMOTHY M. HEALY

One evening when I was dining at 'The Vineyards' with Lord Beaverbrook he said:

"I have a very interesting guest this evening, and an old friend of mine – Tim Healy."

"The first Governor of the Irish Free State?" I asked. "Wasn't he very revolutionary?"

"He was a great Parliamentarian," Max corrected, "a man of fire and vision. Let me tell you a story."

He told me how in the war at the time of the retreat from Mons he was walking with Tim Healy from the House of Commons to the Savoy.

"I was oppressed by a foreboding of disaster," Max said, "for I had seen a despatch which had just arrived from G.H.Q. in France. But Tim was holding forth about the oppression of the Irish and the awful iniquities of British rule. Suddenly I said to him: 'I'm tired of hearing about the grievances of the Irish, let me tell you of the perils of the British Army.'

" 'What are they?' Tim growled.

" 'The C-in-C has said,' Max replied, 'I mean to retire to the sea. If the enemy remains in contact, this will be a very difficult operation. I advise you to look to the defences of Le Havre.' "

Max told me that for a moment there was complete silence. Then he saw the tears streaming down Tim Healy's cheeks, until in a passionate flow of words he dedicated himself before God to the service of the Allied Cause.

"I have known Tim, rebel, agitator, enemy of Great Britain, intimately since that hour," Max finished, "but he has never violated the vow he made to me that evening."

Max also told me how in 1916 he had on Bonar Law's instructions telephoned Tim Healy in Dublin for news of the Easter Rebellion.

"Is there a rebellion?" he asked.

"There is!" replied Tim.

"When did it break out?"

"When Strongbow invaded Ireland!"

"When will it end?"

"When Cromwell gets out of Hell!"

Under Tim Healy, Viceregal Lodge was run with simplicity and

He could speak with a burning passion which could turn disaster into a triumph, and would hold the House of Commons breathless.

dignity. He had exceptionally good taste and collected Waterford glass before other people knew its value and had rare examples of Spanish gold plate.

I was naturally curious and interested to meet this remarkable man. Tim Healy was now over seventy, with a white beard and an expression of melancholy gravity; but when he spoke in his broad, warm Irish brogue, I could still hear the fire behind his words.

Lord Birkenhead wrote of him that year:

> His Parliamentary gifts were individual and extraordinary. He possessed the power of mordant and corrosive sarcasm, the like of which I have never met before. I can still see him standing up to address the House . . . pouring out a long succession of bitter, cruel and wounding insults.

But F.E. added:

> Concealed within this strange personality by his public ferocity are the heart and the temperament of a warm-hearted child.

His Excellency, Max and I set off for Templeton, where Jimmy Dunn was giving a party. It was the usual fantastic, exciting mixture of the grand, the glamorous, the hangers-on and the hung-on-to.

We motored home as dawn was breaking. The old Irishman was full of whisky, and as the Irish always sing in joy or sorrow, sadness or gaiety – he sang.

Most of the songs were, I think, hymns. There were many references to being washed in 'the blood of the Lamb', one about the prodigal son, and a number of dirges about lovers being murdered by the English.

Every so often the Govenor of the Irish Free State would turn to Max and me and demand angrily:

"And why don't ye join in, ye heathens?"

Lovely Lady Lavery from Chicago, invariably wore orchids or Parma violets. Sir John painted her every year.

LADY LAVERY

In 1921 King George and Queen Mary went to Belfast to open the Parliament of the newly partitioned Northern Ireland. In his speech the King said:

> I appeal to all Irishmen to pause, to stretch out the hand of forbearance and conciliation, to forgive and forget, and to join in making for the land they love, a new era of peace, contentment and good will.

This speech coming from the King, had enormous impact. A fortnight later hostilities ceased. The rebel leaders from the South came to London for negotiations, to which Lloyd George brought all his wizardry of persuasiveness. Before the year's end a treaty was signed – the Irish Free State came into being.

One of the people who helped to fashion the Irish Treaty was fascinating Chicago-born Lady Lavery. All soft velvet, sables, scent and big bunches of parma violets, she was irresistibly feminine. Cecil Beaton described her as being like – 'a Luini Madonna – skin of alabaster, hair aflame, eyes huge as a hare's'.

Lady Lavery brought Michael Collins and Winston Churchill together, and one day the history books will show once again the power of the petticoat.

Sir John Lavery painted the leaders of both sides – John Arson and John Redmond – who remarked that they always expected 'to hang together'.

Lady Lavery gave a dinner party for Winston Churchill to meet Michael Collins, the terrorist leader. He was very attractive, and as one lady present said afterwards:

"No wonder he was never caught, all the women must have been glad to hide him."

He had, however, very little sense of humour. One day he was at lunch with the Laverys and Lord Birkenhead was another guest. Hazel had a small Pekinese who was pawing F.E. under the table. She looked down and called the dog:

"Oh, I'm sorry, I thought you were making advances to me," Lord Birkenhead exclaimed.

The big I.R.A. leader towered over him angrily:

"D'ye mean to insult her?" he asked.

"Lord Birkenhead was only joking," Lady Lavery explained quickly.

"I don't understand such jokes," Collins replied.

It was to the Laverys' studio that Michael Collins came after the signing of the Treaty, white and haggard from lack of sleep.

"I have signed some kind of oath," he explained, and added: "Well, I've signed my death warrant!"

He prophesied truly. He was ambushed and killed by the Irregulars in 1922.

Besides being beautiful, Hazel Lavery was sympathetic, charming and adored by many diverse personalities. Tim Healy, Lord Londonderry, James Dunn, Winston Churchill, Ramsay MacDonald and Bernard Shaw were all captivated by her.

Sir John Lavery, who was short and stout, always wore a ribbon four inches wide round his neck as a tie, and a tall top hat square on his square head.

He often stayed with Lord and Lady Londonderry at Mount Stewart, and it was through them he was made a Freeman of Belfast. But he was afraid that his close contacts with Southern Ireland might embarrass them and assured them that he always remembered them in his prayers.

"A form of repayment," he used to say, "which I have often found economical and sometimes impressive."

Sir John faithfully painted his wife every year for the Academy. His pictures had romantic titles – *Hazel in Rose and Gold, Portrait of Hazel in a Mirror, Hazel looking at an Aeroplane.*

Lady Lavery was also depicted on the Irish Free State Bank-notes in 1926 as a colleen with a shawl thrown over her head, leaning on a harp.

Lady Lavery was an artist in her own right, and she gave a joint exhibition with Augustus John. But it is as a charmer she will always be remembered. So many men were in love with her, and women were naturally jealous. She encouraged this by never asking husbands and wives together to her parties.

"Men are never at their best when their wives are there," I heard her say once, "and what woman isn't restricted by the possessive eye of a husband who thinks he is being deceived? No! No! I ask them separately."

But to judge from some of the complaints it was obvious that the wives received unequal portions of fascinating Hazel's hospitality.

In 1921, when the Irish trouble broke out again, Shane Leslie gave a graphic picture of Hazel Lavery at Sir Philip Sassoon's house in Park Lane, compelling Lloyd George to listen for half an hour to her immediate plans for settling the difficulties.

"The Welsh Wizard," he says, "could not have been more polite. She

Douglas Fairbanks

glas with his attractive wife
ary Lee. They have three
hters and six grandchildren.

Douglas and I when we stayed at Broadlands with Lord Mountbatten before he was assassinated. We both loved and admired him more than any other man in the world.

Douglas hiding his fantastic attainments in his colourful and exciting career under a hat. Douglas's autobiography of his extraordinary life in films, the Navy, Diplomacy and public service will be published next year. I expect at least ten volumes!

Gracie Fields

"Gracie Fields is more than a great artiste," C. B. Cochran said. "She is the outstanding artiste of the British Empire. There is nobody as big as Gracie in opera, the legitimate theatre, in cabaret, on the air or in the music hall."

Boris was a rock to Gracie's rolling sea, steadfast, wise, calm and very much in love with his scintillating wife.

Indira Gandhi

The most brilliant and successful woman in the world, Indira Gandhi has not only brains, determination and vision but also a charisma which draws people to her like a magnet. Nobody goes to India without feeling that it touches their heart and soul, as no other country can do. No one meets Indira without being aware that she has a radiance, an inner light which we all seek.

Elinor Glyn

Elinor Glyn passionate and frustrated because her husband was not the ardent lover she longed for, fell wildly, madly in love with the Marquess Curzon of Kedleston. He was a strange, authoritative, dominating man, very conscious of his own importance but everything that Elinor admired and desired. She wrote in her diary:
"O thou great one, calm and wise, accept this my cry of worship. Know that for me thou canst do no wrong. Thou art the mainspring of my life, for whom I would die, for whom I would change my character, curb my instincts, subjugate every wish, give my body and soul, worship blindly... "

really whistled to men, and they obeyed as if it were a whip fashioned of her eyelashes."

Unfortunately even the loveliest of women grow old. Hazel Lavery fought the ravages of age as an artist might do with thick layers of paint.

Lord Berners spread a catty and unkind rumour that the First Lord of the Admiralty, after lunching with Hazel, had entirely revised his plans for camouflaging the Mediterranean Fleet.

It was cruel, but unlike the other fading beauties of the period Hazel's wit and humour sparkled brilliantly until the end.

A cockney from Clapham, she took stardom in her stride.

She had a romantic aura, a magnetic personality, an indescribable glamour.

She was captivating, seductive, enigmatic and mischievous, and without any affectation.

GERTRUDE LAWRENCE

Covered in orchids she would arrive at the stage-door in an Hispano Suiza with a bevy of young men in white ties, top hats and tails.

She would sweep into the Embassy Club glittering like a mermaid in green sequins, or be seen at luncheon wearing a mink coat over grey flannel trousers and look fantastic!

She was a star, she glittered, and was the ideal leading lady for Noel Coward's brittle, bitter-sweet plays.

In real life she was vitally alive with a *joie de vivre* which was like sunshine sparkling on the sea. She was glamour, she was everything every woman longed to be, and every man wanted to possess.

She enchanted her audiences, rekindling in their hearts a faith in imperishable loveliness and romance.

She was overwhelmingly generous with herself and with her extravagances which ran her into bankruptcy. But clothes, furs, jewels were all part of her radiance.

She gave and went on giving – it would have been easier to stop Niagara!

She never took her success for granted, never became spoilt or swollen-headed. She never posed, pretended, or tried to be anything but herself. She always looked and sounded as if she was a child being given a very special treat.

I said to her at a party which would have been a frost without her:

"You make everything you do, Gertie, seem such fun."

"It is fun," she answered. "Sometimes I wake in the night and think it's all a dream and I haven't got anywhere."

"But you have, so there's no need to worry."

"The higher I climb, the further I'll fall!" she laughed.

She was always shadowed by the struggle, the poverty, the dingy 'digs', the 'moonlight flit' when her parents could not pay the rent, the competition she had known on the way up.

She was taking no chances, so every second was precious.

Gertie had the divine spark of vitality, warmth, love and a zeal for living which swept across the footlights and was in her every contact with people.

When she died the lights in London's West End and on Broadway – the most dazzling thoroughfare in 'Show Business' – went out for two minutes in honour of a little cockney girl who captured hearts.

Forced his way to the front by sheer eloquence and assertiveness.

With his wife who always kept very much in the background.

'The Wizard of Wales' in full rhetorical flight when he could charm a bird off a tree.

The only unshingled Member of the House of Commons in 1923.

THE RT. HON. DAVID LLOYD GEORGE
THE 1st EARL LLOYD GEORGE OF DWYFOR

I met Lloyd George in 1924, two years after he had left Downing Street for the last time.

He was still a buoyant, eloquent personality, enormously energetic, with an uncanny ability to read the public mind almost before it had formed itself. But he had lost all popularity, and it was the fashion at that time to abuse and ridicule everything he said or did. Yet no one could help being fascinated by him.

Margot Asquith had said "He could charm the bark off a tree," but this opinion of course was mitigated by J.H. Thomas, the Labour leader, who had said: "You dare not turn your head or blow your nose, or L.G. will trick you."

I heard Lloyd George speak at an enormous meeting at which he was addressing foreign correspondents from all over the world. There was still some fire in his words, still something hypnotic in the way he used his hands and shook his long white hair.

But when we talked, then and on other occasions, I found it hard to credit that people still believed that he was one of the greatest Prime Ministers we had ever had and would make a come-back.

Bob Boothby remembers in 1926 someone in the smoking-room of the House of Commons asking about Lloyd George:

"Can you point to one concrete or permanent piece of work he has ever accomplished?"

Lord Balfour, who had appeared to be asleep, suddenly replied:

"He won the greatest war in history, that really was something of an achievement!"

It was always said in the Twenties how during the war someone asked Lloyd George how soon he wanted something done.

"Tomorrow," he replied. "No, today! Better still, yesterday!"

Lloyd George could be very outspoken. In 1928 the King did not like the idea of the Genoa Conference.

"I suppose," His Majesty said to the Prime Minister, "you will be meeting Lenin and Trotsky."

"Unfortunately Sir," Lloyd George replied, "I am not able to choose whom I meet. A little while ago I had to shake hands with Sami Bey, an Egyptian who was missing the whole of the day and finally traced to a sodomy house in the East End. He was representative of Mustapha Kemal, a man who I understand has grown tired of affairs with women and has taken up unnatural sexual intercourse. I must confess I do not think there is much to choose between these persons and those whom I am forced to meet from time to time in Your Majesty's service."

The King's only reply was to roar with laughter.

Although the Press was far more discreet in those days than it is now, and although there was still a halo of untouchability about Statesmen, Lloyd George's behaviour with women was openly talked about.

Typists in Westminster were said to hurry away at his approach, and the new short skirts just coming in in 1924 were an added enticement to his easily aroused interest in a woman, pretty or otherwise.

His friends didn't hesitate to tease him about it. I remember once at a luncheon party Lloyd George saying about some Bill that was coming before the House:

"We mustn't forget it concerns women. It is essential that we should not forget the women."

There was a guffaw of laughter from everyone present, and someone said:

"That is one thing you are never likely to forget."

Lloyd George took it in good part. He laughed, and I had the feeling he was rather proud of the fact that his friends recognised in him an active masculinity. There was no doubt that a large number of women did like Lloyd George as a man.

One evening he was boasting to me of his successes and I said admiringly:

"You have done so much."

"Do not put it in the past tense," he replied. "In politics there is always tomorrow."

But not for him, he never again held office. Yet he never gave up hope. There were to be flashes of revived activity, moments of brilliance, but these manifestations meant nothing.

When he was seventy-three he said defiantly to Harold Nicolson: "Gladstone went on until he was eighty-five and so shall I!"

THE MARCHIONESS OF LONDONDERRY

Londonderry House was the centre of the political world. Great receptions were held there on the eve of Parliament. Political hostesses were said still to exert a considerable influence over leading Ministers.

Lady Londonderry, who always looked like Boadicea in her chariot, carried the fabulous Londonderry diamond tiara as if it was a crown. In fact, it was not unlike one.

I remember being very overawed by her and the glittery, bejewelled and bedecorated company, as I climbed from the marble hall up the great winding staircase to where at the top she and Lord Londonderry received their guests.

There was a stentorian announcement of names by the Master of Ceremonies in a powdered wig and knee breeches, the rustle of silks, the heat of people crowded together, moving very slowly step by step, the fragrance of scent and flowers, and an occasional whiff of mothballs.

After World War II when the ballroom was let out for parties, we held my daughter Raine's wedding-reception there and I found there was no way of ventilating the long room with its arched ceilings and windowless walls hung with over-life-size Londonderrys.

The Marchioness in her youth had been very gay and wearing a pork-pie hat would ride a bicycle all over London. Once she and a number of friends were chased by a policeman down the Mall because they were riding after dark without lights.

She was still sprightly in the Twenties and had a snake tattooed on one of her ankles. We were always being told about the musical parties she gave every week at Londonderry House to her friends, over whom she had a great influence.

Ironically she made them members of her special 'Ark Club' – a personal zoo where everyone was allotted the name of some animal. She herself was 'Circe', which she had been nicknamed as a child. Lord Londonderry – who was distinguished, handsome, charming and with an irrepressible 'roving eye' – was 'Charlie the Cheetah', Lord Hugh Cecil was 'The Lynx'.

The Prime Minister in the late Twenties, Ramsay MacDonald, was 'The Lion', who because of his attraction to Lady Londonderry was, it was whispered 'saved' from the worse excesses of Socialism.

The young MacDonald was a cartoonist's dream, with rebellious

As Queen Joanna of Scotland in a pageant.

At the opening of Parliament with Lord Newall.

The Londonderry diamonds and chinchilla.

forelock and indignant black moustache, curling like a pair of bicycle handlebars. But 'Gentleman Mac', as he was called by his colleagues, was soon to be more at home with Duchesses than dustmen.

Lady Londonderry could be very frightening. I was at a dance at Londonderry House when a debutante started to stub out a cigarette on the base of one of the marble statues. Lady Londonderry put up her hand and stopped the band.

Controlled and extremely impressive, she walked across the floor and in an icy voice which could be heard all over the room, said to the trembling offender:

"Would you be so kind as to use an ashtray to put out your cigarette!"

The Marchioness's dignity, her influence and authority over the social world is something which will never come again. She loved her power, used it, and hated giving it up.

When the war came and she went to live in Ireland I asked one of her daughters if her mother missed England.

"I think she dreams every night she is standing on top of the staircase with a Prime Minister beside her!" she laughed.

To the politically ambitious that staircase was indisputably a ladder to Heaven!

C.B. Cochran said "She is an incomparable artist with a great creative instinct — she is also a very loyal friend."

In *This Year of Grace* Tilly danced *slowly*! No one for years had dared dance slowly.

TILLY LOSCH

A really lovely girl from Vienna introduced a new note into C.B. Cochran's revue *This Year of Grace*. Instead of dancing quickly and vividly as we had expected, Tilly Losch moved slowly and gracefully like a figure from a stained-glass window to the *Air on a G String* by Bach.

Noel Coward, who had written the revue, was doubtful of this number's success. He begged 'Cockie', as everyone called him, even on the night of production, to take it out. For once in his life he was wrong. 'Gothic', the name of Tilly's dance, was one of the most popular turns in the revue.

Tilly and I travelled to Canada together during the war. There were submarines stalking us, the ship was overrun with children, there weren't enough lifeboats or lifebelts, it was very rough. Tilly lay in bed looking lovely, composed, mysterious and ate caviar.

"It's so uncomfortable when a ship dances," she said.

Tilly had green slanting eyes which gave her an entrancing sphinx-like enigmaticness. She hated black cats, but was herself cat-like in the way she disliked to feel she was being dominated or owned. She did not like people to sit too close to her, she loathed other people to listen to her conversations if she was concentrating on one person.

She hated trams, motor-cars, taxis and aeroplanes! If she had to travel, she liked big ships.

She adored the theatre, which was her love – her passion. She liked swing, Greta Garbo, films and eating. She had to diet, and would discuss it very seriously.

"The bread-and-butter diet – it is good?"

"The banana diet – every day banana, bananas? Oh no!"

"The hay diet – protein one day, starch the next. I should forget!"

"Oh, dear, I do so like my food!"

She craved for Neapolitan ices – one could buy them just outside the theatre; Indian Krapfen, a special chocolate and whipped cream biscuit; stewed beef and horse-radish sauce.

" 'Fey are my ruin, I cannot resist 'fem!"

She could not pronounce 'th'.

Of course, like everyone in the theatre Tilly was superstitious. If she saw a chimney-sweep she had to hold a button of her dress until she saw a white horse – I always blow a kiss to a sweep! Tilly crossed her fingers if she met a cross-eyed man, and would always enter the theatre with her right foot forward.

In 1928 Edward James, son of the famous and beautiful Mrs. James who, for a short time, captivated the vacillating heart of Edward VII, first saw Tilly in *This Year of Grace*.

That the King was Edward's godfather led to a widely held belief that he was in fact his son.

"Because I associated Tilly with beautiful music and beautiful sculpture," Edward said later, "I thought she must have a beautiful soul."

He was too romantic and idealistic to sleep with Tilly before they were married. On their wedding-night she said:

"You're rather a good lover. That makes something a little extra."

He discovered that because of his handsome boyish looks she was convinced that he was a 'queer'.

She was very cruel to him although he lost the £100,000 he spent on a magnificently ambitious theatrical production to try and save their marriage.

After a vitriolic, noisy divorce Tilly married the Earl of Carnarvon, the popular 'Porchie'. She stayed with him for only ten months, then escaped to America.

Here she not only danced, but painted. At the first exhibition of her art she said:

"I feel terrible, as if caught dancing across the stage naked."

She had nightmares in which all her paintings turned into monsters and then came tumbling over her like a pack of cards.

Many years later I went to an exhibition of Oliver Messel's drawings and portraits in London. When I arrived he was talking, as I thought, to a little school-girl with a navy-blue beret on her red hair. It was Tilly!

"How could you look the same as you did forty years ago in *This Year of Grace*?" I asked accusingly. "You have sold your soul to the devil!"

I was wrong! She was a sprite, a will-o'-the-wisp and inhuman – she had no soul.

THE MARCHESE GUGLIELMO MARCONI

He was short, thick-set, and his yachting cap always looked too large for him. He was shy, almost monosyllabic, and rather gauche. I thought he stared at me in what seemed a strange manner until I learnt that he had a glass eye.

He was Italian, born at Bologna, with an Irish mother. He successfully experimented with wireless telegraphy in Italy and England and succeeded in sending signals across the Atlantic in 1901. He was awarded the Nobel Prize in 1909.

I met Billy, as I called him, at Cowes in 1921. The Marconi Experimental Station at Chelmsford had opened the previous year and we had been introduced to headphones which screeched in our ears while we twiddled the knobs, usually unsuccessfully.

I found it far easier to talk on the regular programmes, which I had done twice that year.

In his yacht *Electra*, the wireless equipment which Billy showed me was enormous and completely incomprehensible, so I merely asked ingenuously:

"How does your wireless work?"

"I don't know," he replied.

He always appeared to be a lonely person, and alone at parties. Only his one eye followed me and I knew, as a woman always knows, that he was attracted by me.

The night before the Regatta finished we were dancing on board someone's yacht, I forget whose, and Billy and I walked out on deck.

There were stars in the sky, the lights from the dozens of yachts at anchor were reflected in the water, and the Royal Yacht Squadron was a blaze of light.

It was breathtakingly beautiful, with the gramophone playing behind us, and music wafted on the warm air from every other yacht, very romantic.

I stood at the rail looking and listening and Billy stood beside me. I knew he was struggling to say something, I could feel him vibrating emotionally.

I waited, then a voice from the Saloon shouted:

"Come on, Barbara, we're going ashore."

"I'm coming," I replied.

I turned to the man beside me.

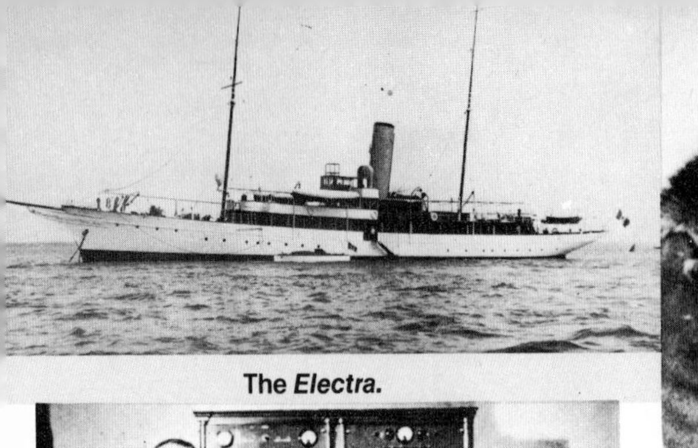

The *Electra*.

With Pope Pius XI in the Vatican.

With his wife who he married in 1927.

With his early apparatus.

Marconi as I knew him in 1923.

With King Victor Emmanuel III a
Mussolini.

"Are you coming with us?"
"No, I'm going back to *Electra*."
"Then, 'good-bye', it's been fun meeting you."
"Good-bye, Barbara – will you write to me?"
"Perhaps, but I'm a bad letter writer."
"Then will you think of me?"
"When I am listening to your wireless."
As I was carried towards the shore in a launch I looked back and saw Billy standing alone on deck. I waved, but he didn't respond.
I never saw him again, but what can you do about an Italian who is inarticulate?

I took Queen Marie, Prince Tomislav and Prince Andre 1944, to visit McCorquodales who were printing the ra books and clothing coupons.

King Alexander of Yugoslavia assassinated in Marseilles, October 1934.

EX-QUEEN MARIE OF YUGOSLAVIA

In the war I found an ex-Queen isolated in a small village in Bedfordshire. Queen Marie was the wife of the assassinated Alexander of Yugoslavia. She and her son, King Peter, and his two younger brothers, Tomislav and Andrei, were all exiled from their country.

Queen Marie was having a dreary time confined in a house with only a lady-in-waiting and two Yugoslav servants for company.

Because as the only female Welfare Officer to the Armed Services in the county I was trying to find entertainments and interests for enormous numbers of W.A.A.F. personnel in dozens of secret stations, she was a godsend!

I had already found that under the name of 'Recreational Occupations' I could buy rayon, georgette and crepe-de-chine for cami-knickers. I had inaugurated a pool of white wedding-dresses at the War Office, but a Queen would also, I thought, raise the morale in the very, very hush-hush stations where the women were fed up and bored!

Stout because she never took any exercise, but with a sweet expression, Queen Marie was the second daughter of King Ferdinand and Queen Marie of Romania. She was pretty placid, and very unlike her dazzlingly beautiful, passionate mother, or her unpredictable brother King Carol, with his hopeless weakness for women.

King Alexander, with whom Queen Marie had been very happy, was shot dead in Marseilles in 1934 by a Bulgarian hired assassin in the pay of a Croat organisation.

I took the Queen round dozens of R.A.F. stations, convalescent camps and maintenance factories. The R.A.F. and A.T.S. were thrilled as a Queen was something new to talk about. She, on the other hand, was delighted to have something to do. It was a very pale reflection of her former glory – but when I took her from station to station she was, for a few hours, the centre of attraction.

There were bows and curtseys, and she walked for miles while her lady-in-waiting and I trailed behind!

Monarchy without thrones and many without money were one of the rather pathetic spectacles of the period – rather like the White Russians after 1917! One curtseyed lower to them and 'Sir'ed' or 'Ma'am'ed' them more punctiliously because they were out of date, a relic of the days before the war 'rolled up the map of Europe'.

I once asked the Queen what she felt about the contrast between her past life and her present one. For a moment her eyes expressed all she never said in words.

"When there is no future," she replied quietly, "and the past has gone, one accepts the present."

ELSA MAXWELL

I disliked Elsa Maxwell because although she was at least a foot shorter than I am, she was always looking over my head to see if there was someone smarter and more important she might be talking to.

She was ugly, short, dumpy, ebullient, egotistic, thick-skinned and bounced off a snub like a football. But I was forced to admire her boundless zest for life, her originality, her enjoyment of the ridiculous.

She never drank alcohol and yet she could infuse a champagne atmosphere in a way no one else has ever managed to do before or since.

Elsa was an American. Her father was a non-conformist Scottish newspaper correspondent, her mother was the daughter of a doctor and she was born during a perfomance of *Mignon* in a theatre box in Keokuk, Iowa.

At five years old she sang for Adelina Patti, and she developed the extraordinary musical talent of having a perfect pitch which enabled her to play any classical or popular selection in any key after hearing it once.

Caruso, Gershwin, Rubinstein and Kreisler all agreed it was impossible for her to strike a false note.

She became an accompanist and toured South Africa. She composed many successful songs, but it was something which happened when she was twelve which decided her strange and unique fate.

In San Francisco the Maxwells had a four-roomed flat. Across the street was the grand mansion belonging to Senator James G. Fair, and Elsa was close friends with his daughters.

The Senator planned a party for Teresa his eldest girl with an orchestra from New York. Elsa asked her mother excitedly:

"What are you going to wear?"

"You don't have to worry about that," her mother replied, "we are too poor to be asked."

Elsa sat at the window that night, too proud to cry, watching the gorgeously dressed guests arriving at the Fair mansion.

"It was the first time," she said, "I ever realised money was a social weapon. I swore to myself I would give great parties all over the world – I didn't know how or when – to which everyone would want to come, but the rich would be invited only if they had something more important to offer than money."

When Elsa Maxwell's Scavenger Hunts, Murder Parties and Fancy-Dress Balls became the rage in Paris, London and New York, she

"This record of a shoot in Hungary," Elsa wrote, "always gives me a laugh."
Elsa weighed 193 lbs and was too busy giving parties to slim.

With Maria Callas, who wrote pathetically to Elsa: "God knows, I am human. Maybe I am too proud to show it."

Elsa as Barnum with Gloria Swanson and Lily Pons, and riding a motorbike for the benefit of the Bob Club, St. Moritz. Elsa would go anywhere, do anything if it was socially 'smart

would think of her first exposure to snubbing and the resentment which had choked her.

But how brilliant she was! In Paris the manager of the Casino de Paris put in a riot call for the police when two Scavenger Hunters rushed on to the stage, grabbed one of Mistinguett's slippers and then took the rest of her shoes from her dressing-room, so that she was forced to finish her act in bare feet.

Elsa watched with John Barrymore the fires caused by the San Francisco earthquake in 1906. She ran a night club in Paris with Edward Molyneux, the famous dress designer. She promoted Monte Carlo as a summer resort, she was first to congratulate Franklyn D. Roosevelt on his election to the Presidency in 1932.

She helped, quarrelled with, and made it up with the Duchess of Windsor.

She fell over when she curtseyed to Queen Mary who helped her to her feet, she knew all the English Dukes, most of the European nobility, the Greek ship-owners and American Presidents.

Noel Coward said that 'she curdled her own personality with too much *crème-de-la-crème*'; but her parties were always fantastic, always unexpected.

Cecil Beaton wrote in one of his clever biographies:

> Miss Maxwell's real ambition is never satisfied until she has made the most distinguished people appear undistinguished. To this purpose she invented many clever 'stunt' parties at which members of the aristocracy of Italy, France and England, together with politicians and statesmen, were 'knocked off their pedestals'.

At her first pompous party in London Elsa made her self-assured guests sit on the floor and blow a feather off a sheet! One of her most publicised evenings was a 'farmyard' affair, where her sophisticated friends appeared as rustics, and milked an artificial cow for champagne.

Since Elsa Maxwell had more character and intelligence than many of her guests, she succeeded in her objective. The pictures that inevitably appeared after each party made her victims appear extremely foolish.

Elsa would have been the first to admit she was getting back at Senator James G. Fair!

The Press at first thought Mosley was an energetic young man injecting his vitality into the British. They soon realised their mistake.

His lovely first wife Cynth
daughter of the Marques
Curzon of Kedleston.

SIR OSWALD MOSLEY

Oswald Mosley was born with a silver spoon in his mouth. Heir to a baronetcy, tall, handsome, rich, elegant, he was first elected to Parliament as a Conservative in 1918.

But a bad fairy at his christening gave him a pugnacity which destroyed his judgement and often his decent feelings for people. He began to live only for opposition and when he could not find one, he created one.

He joined the Labour Party and became Chancellor for the Duchy of Lancaster, but they were not progressive enough to suit him and when I knew him first he was organising a mass of Left Wing discontents.

Still unsatisfied he decided in 1931 to start a new Party 'for action'.

Most of Mosley's personal friends, who always called him 'Tom', were, however, of the opinion that to start a new Party at the moment, was suicidal to his career, for he would in time undoubtedly be a powerful element in the Labour Government.

'Nigs' Ratendone, later the second Marquis of Willingdon, told me how, after Sir Oswald had announced that he intended to start the 'New Party' he was taken ill and his wife, Lady Cynthia, rang up to say that she was taking him for a short holiday to the South of France.

"Keep him there," Nigs implored her. "If any man had a second chance Tom's got one now."

But his advice was disregarded, and twenty-two candidates for the New Party lost their deposits in the 1931 Election, the best known among them being the Hon. Harold Nicolson. Eventually losing its Labour supporters the New Party ended as a purely Fascist movement.

Everyone loved Cynthia Mosley. It was, perhaps, inevitable that both she and her sister, Baroness Ravensdale, should be Socialists after an upbringing of pomp and pomposity with their brilliant but overpowering father, George Nathaniel, the first Marquess Curzon of Kedleston.

Cynthia, who was beautiful, had a great sense of humour. When she told her father that she was engaged to Oswald Mosley he reached for Debrett. She took it out of his hand and gave him the telephone-book.

She and Sir Oswald were the first husband and wife to sit in the House of Commons together.

I used to meet and see 'Tom' Mosley night after night on the balcony of the fashionable Café de Paris where one did not have to wear evening-dress. He would be having supper with a very pretty friend of mine who was soft, sweet and feminine.

He always looked dark, sinister and aggressively masculine. He seldom smiled and when we talked he would stand, staring with black eyes as if he looked into a fathomless future.

One evening after I and the man I was with walked away I said dramatically:

"Tom is a seething volcano and I am sure when he stood at the crossroads he took the downward path to hell."

"Nonsense!" my companion replied, "Tom is a very clever chap. You only dislike him because he has no small talk."

Cynthia, whom everyone loved, died of peritonitis in 1933 and three years later Tom married Diana, one of the beautiful, brilliantly witty Mitford sisters. To keep their marriage secret they were married in the drawing room of Goebbels's house in Berlin and spent the evening with him and Hitler.

The rest is history. In 1940 the Mosleys were arrested. Tom was taken to Brixton Prison and Diana to Holloway. They were imprisoned in ghastly conditions for three-and-a-half years.

I can never hear or think of Tom Mosley without remembering a play called: *The Postman Never Knocks Twice.*

He did knock twice for Tom, but he wouldn't listen.

LADY LOUIS MOUNTBATTEN
THE COUNTESS OF MOUNTBATTEN OF BURMA

Granddaughter of one of the richest men in the world, goddaughter of Edward VII, wife of the most romantic hero of our time and one of the great women of the century, Edwina and I were the same age.

Her father, Lord Mount Temple was a great friend of my father and mother, her stepmother used to stay with us when I was a child.

Edwina was always to me a fairy-tale figure. Her beauty because she was so animated always eclipsed that of every other woman in a room. She had deep blue eyes which could have an unexpected tenderness and expression in them.

She was the most acclaimed beauty in the Twenties, but she broke out of her gilded cage to work among lepers, to kiss the untouchable Indian babies, to clean up with her own hands filthy P.O.W. huts and to leave a legend of kindness, understanding and efficiency behind her wherever she went.

One night in the war, when Edwina was staying with me in our tiny thatched cottage in Bedfordshire, we sat up late as Edwina told me how she travelled up to the front lines of Burma and Chungking where she visited hospitals, medical centres, convalescent homes, blood-banks and canteens, inspecting everything, shaking hands and talking to everyone, including the India sepoys and cleaners, which was apparently a flagrant breach of etiquette.

She even travelled third-class half across India in a troop train to see for herself the state of the lavatories and the lack of water. During the night she found the overcrowding so ghastly that she climbed into a luggage rack.

"Was that better?" I asked.

"Much better," replied Edwina. "It was like sleeping in a hammock!"

Once at Arakan, her route lay across a river and the bridge had been destroyed. She swam it!

She told me, too, how in one Chinese hospital the cleanliness and apparent good health of the patients momentarily deceived her. Then evading her escorts she slipped around the back of the building to find filthy dirty huts crammed with unattended sick and badly wounded men where they had been hidden.

She adored her lovely red-haired sister Mary, and I loved her too, so as Edwina rushed off to some inaccessible part of the world, she would

Her wedding in 1922 to Lord Louis Mountbatten, R.N.

With me at my St. John Ambulance exhibition in 1945 which she opened.

always say: "Look after Mary," which I tried to do.

Then on 21 February 1959 at seven o'clock in the morning the telephone rang beside my bed. As it was Sunday I couldn't think who could be waking me. When I lifted the receiver I found it was Mary, desperately upset.

She told me that Dickie Mountbatten had just telephoned to tell her that Edwina had been found dead in British North Borneo.

It didn't seem possible that anyone so vital, so energetic, should die. Only the month before, when we were staying at Six Mile Bottom with Mary, I had given Edwina a lecture saying she was doing too much.

"We are the same age," I said, "and I know that I couldn't fly to India for breakfast, inspect three hospitals, review the local division of the St. John Ambulance Brigade and fly on to do the same thing in another part of the world. You must take life a little easier!"

She laughed, but afterwards she had written me a letter saying:

> I promise you this is my last marathon. After that I will take my vitamins, grease my face and try and do all the things you have told me to do.

It seemed impossible that Edwina was dead . . . that she would not be there to turn to in all the many troubles in which she had been an unfailing tower of strength!

I had telephoned her so often in some distant part of the world when there were family problems or difficulties in the St. John Ambulance Brigade.

It must have often seemed very trivial to her – some high-up official had been rude to a junior officer, who had threatened to resign; the County Commissioner was upset, and he too was thinking of leaving! All small things in themselves, they were never too small for Edwina.

"Don't worry, darling, I will see to it," she would say.

Looking back I see now what this must have meant when she was coping with the world-shattering events of the Partition of India, crowds of starving refugees, an earthquake in Greece, cholera somewhere else! Yet she always had time. Now we were to be without her!

It was not until I went to India that I realised what an incredible job the Mountbattens had done.

It is easy to sit at home and talk about 'Partition', but when one sees the enormity of the continent itself, when one realises the millions of people involved, their different creeds, castes and faiths, all conflicting one with the other, one begins to understand a little of what had been achieved.

And despite the personal cost in death, in disruption, in poverty and in desolation, the Indians had one and all respected, admired and loved the Mountbattens.

As Pandit Nehru said to Edwina in his farewell speech when the Mountbattens left India:

> Wherever you have gone, you have brought solace, and you have brought hope and encouragement. Is it surprising, therefore, that the people of India should love you and look up to you as one of themselves, and should grieve that you are going.

Who could ask for a greater tribute?

In India the two Houses of Parliament stood in silence when Edwina died. The St. John Ambulance Brigade will never forget her, nor will those who worked with her in the Save the Children Fund. Edwina's work will go on. But most of all she will survive as a legend in India. She gave its people her whole heart and they will never forget.

Pandit Nehru wrote to me two days before Edwina's Memorial Service in Westminster Abbey. In his letter he said:

> It is difficult to realise that Edwina has gone. She was so full of life and vitality and one could not associate death with her. I have to remind myself often that she is not coming back. And yet, the manner of her death was typical of her. She died as she had lived, full of life and energy and devoted to the work she had undertaken.

I do not associate death with Edwina because she lives in what she achieved – she linked people of every caste, and creed, of every colour and nationality together with the unbreakable tie of love.

ADMIRAL OF THE FLEET THE EARL MOUNTBATTEN OF BURMA

I agreed with the Prince of Wales when he said that Lord Mountbatten was 'the most interesting, exciting, knowledgeable and fascinating man alive'.

The Prince, however, forgot to say he was also the most amusing and the most inventive.

Everyone knows about Lord Mountbatten's amazing success in the Royal Navy, his bravery in bringing home HMS *Kelly* on a ninety-two-hour tow under constant enemy air attack, his victories as Supreme Allied Commander of the South East Asia Command, that he was the last Viceroy and having given the Indians their independence they paid him the unique compliment of asking him to remain on as their first 'Head of State'.

But what so many people do not know is that he could have made a separate career for himself as an inventor.

His father, Admiral of the Fleet Prince Louis of Battenberg (first Marquess of Milford Haven) invented the Battenberg Course Indicator in the early 1890s. This was an ingenious instrument which solved the problem of triangles of velocity mechanically and quickly.

It soon became a basic universal invention used in every Navy, both when taking up station on a moving ship at sea and in fire control instruments, and when the Air Force came along, they used it for their bomb sights.

His son Dickie invented something on the same lines, known as the Mountbatten Station Keeping Equipment.

This was fitted in over sixty cruisers and destroyers before and during World War II and made it far easier for ships to keep close station on each other when in mass formations at any speed.

It was very popular both with the officers handling the ship on the bridge and those in the engine room.

He had several other Naval inventions such as a small sub-focal signalling shutter to use inside a big searchlight signalling projector, a quick action torpedo grab to pick up torpedoes after an exercise at twice the normal speed, and a new type of torpedo sight based on a three-dimensional cam design.

He also thought of the Mountbatten Course Ruler which simply took the compass rose from the chart and put it on the transparent ruler

From the moment Louis Mountbatten knocked off Queen Victoria's spectacles as she held him in her arms he could get away with anything. Including being the most revolutionary and adored Viceroy India ever had.

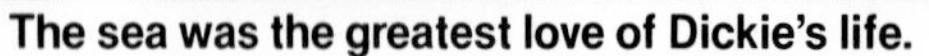

The sea was the greatest love of Dickie's life.

Winning by his original method of rowing i 1935.

which made it easier and quicker to lay off exact courses and bearings.

In November 1932 the Commander-in-Chief of the Mediterranean Fleet sent for Dickie Mountbatten and said:

"As you know King George V is going to broadcast to the Empire on Christmas Day. I want you to arrange that every man in the fleet will hear his voice."

Dickie at once pointed out that there wasn't a single piece of equipment supplied by His Majesty's Navy which would enable the King's voice to be heard.

He was then given a large sum from the Commander-in-Chief's contingency fund to devise a new short-wave radio receiver which he put on a high point in Malta to receive the new B.B.C. short-wave transmitter direct.

To this he coupled a powerful transmitter on a medium frequency in one of the ships which could transmit a signal which everybody could receive not only in the ships, but also ashore. They also had to produce proper loudspeakers which weren't supplied by the Service.

The whole operation was a knockdown success and from it were born two important things.

Firstly loudspeaker systems were fitted throughout ships by which orders could be passed instantly, instead of the Bosun's Mate having to round and pipe vocally on all decks and, which is far more exciting, it started the Forces Broadcasting Service.

Dickie also arranged for his staff to convert the silent cinema projectors of the big ships in the Mediterranean Fleet to 'talkies' at a cost of less than a tenth of new sound projectors.

He then started the Royal Naval Film Corporation which buys prints at a fair price from the big film companies and lends them out at a small rental to sea-going ships. This facility is a tremendous morale booster, particularly in Polaris submarines who, during their regular two-month diving patrols, can have a different film show every night they are at sea.

During the war Dickie invented a special form of violet pink light grey paint which became known as 'Mountbatten Pink'. This made ships much more difficult to see in hazy conditions.

His inventions were not all confined to the Service. In 1979 he drove me in his 1924 Rolls-Royce, a Silver Ghost with a Barker Cabriolet body. He designed the body himself and it was the first streamlined Rolls-Royce.

He arranged for the headlamps to be made both to dip and also to track with the front wheels so that on a winding road one had the advantage of the headlamps showing the direction in which one was actually going, as on a motorcycle. It was fifty years before Citroen copied his idea.

Dickie could turn his mind to anything. Edwina had a number of pieces of beautiful jewellery designed by him, which we all admired and envied.

Dickie's inventiveness took a different turn and was not only concerned with actual gadgets but the way of 'doing' things. For instance when he was in command of the destroyer *Wishart* he changed the conventional stroke for pulling or rowing whalers in Regattas.

He cut out the beginning and end of the stroke and the shorter stroke enabled his crews to tow at forty strokes to the minute instead of thirty-two. Little wonder that the *Wishart* won all the whaler races and the overall Regatta 'Cock'.

He applied the same technique to gunnery competitions. In those days the vogue was to fire off as many broadsides as possible, up to nine or ten a minute with 4.7 inch guns. He reduced the rate of fire and concentrated on greater accuracy in hitting the target.

This didn't make him very popular with the other ships in the Fleet but he won the gunnery trophy too!

It was Dickie who conceived the idea of using faradism to cure lameness in horses. A great friend of his, a well known Naval Physiotherapist, used to keep the polo players of the Navy Blue Jackets team fit by giving them faradic treatment for their injuries.

It was so successful that Dickie suggested that he should apply the same treatment to the horses. His friend demurred but Dickie pulled rank and persuaded him to use it on the ponies' legs and they were cured very quickly, in a way that had never been thought of before.

It took a long time before the Veterinary fraternity would accept this revolutionary type of treatment but it is now used throughout the world.

When years later I told Dickie proudly I had a new machine for strained muscles, in the Health Movement, and he said he had invented it for polo ponies, I didn't believe him!

In 1936 Brook House, which had been built on the site of the enormous Park Lane Mansion belonging to Edwina's grandfather Sir Ernest Cassel, was completed. The first six floors were all flats to be let but the seventh and eighth were designed as a Penthouse for Edwina and Dickie.

Set back like a country house, it had an exceptional number of rooms big enough to give a party for over 600.

I remember lunching with the Mountbattens soon after they had started to move into the new Penthouse. Dickie's sister, Queen Louise of Sweden and the King and several other distinguished guests were present but we all ate informally off card tables with oddments of china as most of the furniture had not been unpacked!

Dickie had arranged for the first express lift in England to be installed in Brook House which went direct from a private entrance to the seventh or eighth floors and worked locally between the two floors.

Admiral of the Fleet
The Earl Mountbatten of Burma

Driven by a burning ambition to vindicate his father, Admiral of the Fleet Prince Louis of Battenberg, Dickie's rage forged his character. It drove him into a holy war against the world in which he never relaxed, never forgot until he took his father's place as First Lord of the Admiralty.

"The Supremo" had an obsession with detail and when he officially retired and was busier than ever, he missed nothing! Kimberley, his adoring and adored labrador had his health, food and figure watched carefully.

At Helfex with me in 1978. He opened my Health Food Conference and because of his patronage the exports trebled. Everyone speaks of his courage, loyalty, brilliant intelligence and far sighted vision, but they forget his sense of humour.
When he was assassinated those who loved him missed most his happy spontaneous laughter and a Joy of Living which was infectious.

The Countess Mountbatten of Burma

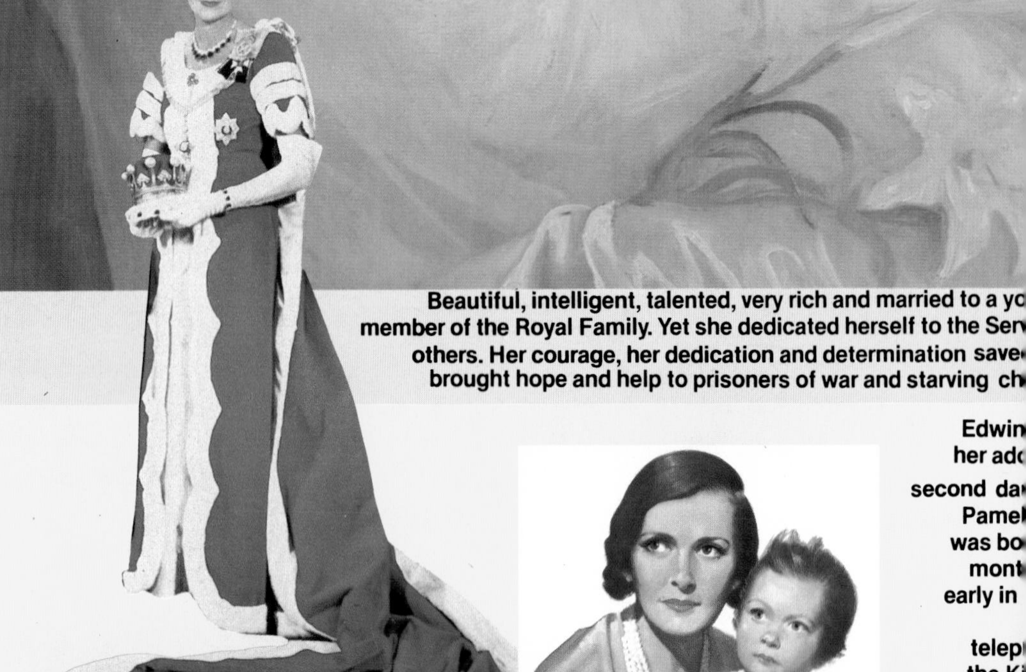

Beautiful, intelligent, talented, very rich and married to a yo
member of the Royal Family. Yet she dedicated herself to the Serv
others. Her courage, her dedication and determination save
brought hope and help to prisoners of war and starving ch

In her Peeress' robes but she was more at home in the uniform of the St. John Ambulance Brigade, in which she travelled all over the world.

Edwin
her add
second da
Pamel
was bo
mont
early in

telep
the Ki
help. He
num
soldie
surro
the hot
refuse
any
includi
D

Gordon Selfridge

Gordon Selfridge first saw the Dolly Sisters, two attractive Hungarians with liquid eyes doing a cabaret turn in the Kit-Cat Club. He was so obsessively infatuated with Jenny that he could refuse her nothing. He bought an interest in the Casino at Le Touquet and gave her unlimited credit. She once played from Friday until Tuesday, winning £700,000 at one moment and losing it all again before she staggered exhausted back to her hotel.

Jenny wore a solitaire diamond ring the size of a walnut and diamond bracelets (we called them service stripes) from her wrists to her elbows.

But the gambling could not last for ever. When Gordon Selfridge could not pay Jenny's debts of £90,000, and she had already cost him two million, she committed suicide.

Dorothy Squires

This is a very unusual photograph taken on the stage of the Palladium with Dorothy making the whole audience sing to me:— "If You Were the Only Girl in the World." I am in the Royal Box and I was very touched by such a tribute from a professional to an amateur.
The Palladium was filled with Dorothy's fans, who every year expect to have the opportunity to show her their love and loyalty in whichever theatre she takes for the evening.
After the performance in her dressing- room you can see Dorothy with me and my son Glen. Half hidden in the background is Norman Newell who produced my Album of Love Songs. I am the only woman ever to sing her first Album at the age of 78.

Unfortunately the lift always obeyed the first order of any button. When Queen Mary came to see the new Penthouse in the early days Dickie waited for Her Majesty in the private ground floor hall with the lift held.

Alas, someone not knowing about the Royal visit, pressed the button on the eighth floor.

When Queen Mary got in the lift Dickie pressed the button for the seventh floor but it obeyed the original summons and the Queen arrived on the eighth floor which was in the throes of being decorated! The Press had a field day with the story!

Dickie and Edwina had diffused lighting which was very new in those days and also projectors hidden in the walls with beams which could shine an exact light on to separate pictures. I believe Brook House was the first house in England to be fitted with these 'spotlights'.

Dickie wore the first zip fastener on a pair of trousers. He persuaded his cousin, Edward the Prince of Wales to copy him. It was not a success!

The very first time they both went out to a restaurant half an hour away from Biarritz, where they were staying, H.R.H. could not come out of the cloakroom, as his zip had stuck. He gave up his dinner, went home in disgust and had the zips taken out of his trousers.

Dickie was also the first man to wear elastic laces on his shoes so he didn't have to do them up, and the first to wear permanent suspenders woven into the socks to save having separate suspenders.

But the purpose of this book is to show the magnetic power of those who lead and achieve success. Dickie had this to such a fantastic degree, that it is almost indescribable.

Sometimes to touch his hand was like receiving a small electric shock and the force, when he used it in a dangerous situation or because he had to convince people what he believed was right, was overwhelming.

It was this which gave him a way with men which made them trust, revere and follow him wherever he went. His magnetic vitality drew those who followed him and he also had humanity which made them love and trust him.

It was not surprising that everyone he knew from the Royal Family to his most insignificant friends turned to him for advice.

He never failed to help and only his personal staff knew how many letters he received from all over the world from those who had served with him and who knew he would have still listened to their troubles.

Few outstanding leaders had Dickie's wonderful gift for laughter. He instilled his sense of humour into his men and even after the *Kelly* had sunk beneath their feet, the survivors still found the courage to laugh and joke.

When he went to the Front to talk to the Army in Burma he staggered them by saying:

"I hear you call yourself the 'Forgotten Army' and say this is the Forgotten Front. I have come today to tell you that you are not the Forgotten Army and this is not the Forgotten Front – nobody has even heard of you!"

He then went on:

"But they are going to hear about you now, because this is what we are going to do."

It is not surprising that the Army Commander 'Bill' Slim said:

"When you see Dickie it is good for your morale."

Dickie had the aura of victory about him and his unquenchable optimism and his incorrigible youthful sense of high adventure made him the hero which every man dreams of being, and whom every girl would like to meet.

Winston Churchill put him in charge of preparing the invasion of Europe when he became Chief of Combined Operations in 1943. He decided the only feasible place to land was in Normandy but all the senior Generals, many of them a generation or more older than him, were determined that the Pas de Calais area was best.

Dickie stuck to his guns and when finally the German Generals came to the conclusion that the attack was bound to be in the Pas de Calais area, Hitler sent twenty-five Divisions there to meet them.

The Germans were completely thrown off balance when the landing took place in Normandy.

In Burma too he turned things upside down. The very first speech he made to the Headquarters of the Army Command and the Tactical Air Force staff shook them. He said:

"I hear that every time the Japanese outflank you and cut off your lines of communication you always fall back on to your base so as not to lose your supply line. In future you will stay where you are and fight. I will supply you by air."

He did not have enough transport aircraft to carry out his promise, so he took them off the American Transport aircraft supplies into China which came under his control. He did this on two occasions and incurred the wrath of Roosevelt for doing so, but he won through!

He was always very conscious of the importance of good health. He was horrified by the fact that for every one battle casualty, 120 men were in hospital with tropical diseases. He assembled the finest tropical disease experts he could get and soon had conquered the problem to the extent that the figure finally came down to one in six.

Having tackled morale and malaria, he turned to the next problem – the Monsoon.

He told his Army and Air Commanders that he had discovered that during the five months of the dreadful drenching west Monsoon, both sides stopped fighting and flying altogether.

He said that during the next Monsoon the Allies would go on flying, fighting and marching and thus steal a vital advantage. This was the turning point in the Burma Campaign.

Only Dickie Mountbatten could have brought the Indian Empire to an end in such a dignified and honourable way after forty years of agitation and repression. Not with the sound of cannon and gunfire, but with the genuine love which he and Edwina felt for the Indian people and they for them.

This love and faith in the Indians was clearly demonstrated when they flew to Peshawar to see for themselves the troubles in the North West Frontier province.

On arrival they were greeted with the news that a huge crowd of 70,000 to 100,000 aggressive Pathan tribesemen were about to march on Government House. Dickie and Edwina immediately went along to face the crowd, many of them armed and waving the illegal green and white flag of Pakistan and shouting *'Pakistan Zindabad'*.

Edwina told me what a hair-raising moment it was as she and Dickie stood on a bank, seeing the seething crowd beneath them.

"It was Dickie's supreme self-confidence," she said, "which turned the tide for, instead of against us."

But I know it was the power he gave out in time of danger which was irresistible. The chant of the Pathans changed to 'Mountbatten *Zindabad*' and for nearly half an hour Dickie and Edwina stood waving to the crowd.

In his seventy-ninth year he struck out on a brave new venture and opened his Hampshire home, Broadlands near Romsey, to the public. This beautiful house, originally built in the sixteenth century and then refaced in the Palladian style in the eighteenth century by the Second Lord Palmerston, is one of the finest country houses in England.

But perhaps its greatest attraction was its owner.

I asked an expert on historic houses whether Broadlands would attract many visitors and he replied:

"Can you imagine what it would have been like if Wellington had opened his house after the Battle of Waterloo? Well, this is even more exciting because Lord Mountbatten has had the advantage of worldwide television coverage of his life and time."

So we get back to what the Prince of Wales said of this extraordinary man, who has done everything and done it not only outstandingly well, but with great imagination, insight, vision and something inexplicable.

All the people in this book had or have it to some degree but in Dickie it was a vital, compelling power. I could feel it as the men who served under him felt it, but I cannot explain it, I can only say it radiated irresistibly from him.

Because of it until he was assassinated in 1979 he was not only 'the most interesting, exciting, knowledgeable, fascinating man alive' but the most magnetic.

Nehru with his grandchild Rajiva. He was always thinking ahead. To him it was tomorrow which counted, not yesterday.

With his beloved pandas. "Tomorrow," he said, "they go to the hills." And the hills meant all the things he could not do.

1958. My first visit to India. Lt. to Rt. Edwina Mountbatten, Indira Gandhi, Pamela Mountbatten, Me and Pandit Nehru

PANDIT NEHRU

The Prime Minister's House where Ian and I had lunch in 1958 was formerly the Residence of the British Commander-in-Chief in Delhi. It was like every British Residence of any importance in every land that the British had ruled.

Indira told me that when she and her father moved in, staring down from the walls of the chief rooms were life-size portraits of stern Generals resplendent in their gold-braided uniforms.

She felt them watching her every movement, criticising her every unspoken thought. She had them all taken down and despatched to the Ministry of Defence.

All I saw on the wall was a valuable Chinese painting – hung crooked.

The garden was a riot of English flowers. Great beds of pansies, crimson and purple sweet williams, and a glowing mass of antirrhinums planted by Memsahibs who were homesick.

Inside the house was exactly as the British must have left it. Chintz curtains, comfortable low chairs, closely fitted carpets and heavy, unimaginative mahogany furniture.

My son and I were given a choice of orange or mango juice. There was no alcohol of any sort in the Prime Minister's house and he was trying to make prohibition effective all over India.

There were only six of us to lunch – Nehru and his quiet, rather shy daughter Indira, Edwina Mountbatten and her daughter Pamela, Ian and I.

I was surprised to see how small Nehru was. His pictures, which one still finds in every airport and on practically every wall in India, make him appear a large man. In actual fact he could not have been much over five feet five inches. His hair was grey and he looked all of his sixty-nine years.

"It is fifty-one years since I was at Harrow," he told Ian who was at the same school. "It is a very long time ago."

His education in England at Harrow, Trinity College, Cambridge and at the Inner Temple, left him as he said:

"A queer mixture of East and West, out of place everywhere, at home nowhere."

But he was to take over India, torn, divided but free from the last Viceroy, and say on the air in his disarming fashion:

"We are little men serving a great cause. But because the cause is great something of the greatness falls upon us."

The morning we lunched with him Nehru had said in Congress:

"I hope that we shall avoid saying things which will add to the already large fund of bitterness and ill-will in this world."

To him the past is past.

"You were imprisoned for fourteen years of your life," I said to him. "You were beaten and insulted. Don't you hate the British who did this to you?"

Nehru shook his head.

"Does it matter tomorrow?" he asked.

The key to his whole outlook was the future, and I had the idea that it kept him awake at night.

"We must build every type of house for every type of people," he said to me when I congratulated him on the new buildings going up round Delhi.

India's housing problem seemed to me just an echo of what we had been coping with in England since the war, because however many houses were built the population kept growing and the demands seemed insatiable.

After lunch, not I thought a very sustaining one for a tired man, in a very English dining room with dark wood walls, blue curtains and imitation Hepplewhite chairs, we visited the Prime Minister's Himalayan pandas. These brown and white, sharp-eyed little animals, called Bhimsa and Poma, were lying panting in the heat but we were told, were being taken to the hills at Naini Tal the next day.

When we left, Pandit Nehru escorted us to the door. It was part of the exquisite good manners that one finds everywhere in India, that the host not only meets one at the door on arrival, but he stands on the step until one has departed.

A thousand times since I have thought of his penetrating eyes smouldering with a visionary fire, the vibrations exuding from him and his deep voice saying quietly:

"Does it matter tomorrow?"

THE COUNTESS OF OXFORD (MARGOT ASQUITH)

To me Mrs. Asquith – afterwards Lady Oxford – with her big nose, coarse grey hair brushed upwards from her sharp-angled face, her dark eyes, spindly legs and bony shoulders, looked like a witch in modern dress.

She had a quick wit, but was very superior in her attitude. She was also impatient and intolerant of stupidity, and this often prevented her from appreciating those who were not fools but merely shy.

Margot Asquith's autobiography had shocked my mother's generation. She had not only revealed intimacies about her friends, 'the Souls', she had also said that several distinguished men were in love with her! This was considered very indiscreet. Lytton Strachey, the literary giant, disliked the book so much he refused to review it.

Margot Asquith wished to be outrageous, provocative, and permanently in the limelight. She was witty and one of the great personalities of the period, but she had to attract attention. During the war it had been rumoured she was in the pay of the Germans and she was booed in the streets.

Extraordinary stories were circulated about the Asquiths, such as that they had shares in Krupps. As Margot related:

> It was said openly that from attic to basement my household, my friends and my family were pro-German. When Lord Kitchener was drowned I was inundated with anonymous and insulting letters accusing me of having signalled from some secret place in the North Sea to a German submarine that was supposed to have sunk the *Hampshire*.

She would recount this experience dramatically, but one could not help feeling from the glint in her eye that she had enjoyed the excitement of being a martyr.

Mr. Asquith, the ex-Prime Minister who always seemed in the Twenties rather dull to the outside public in comparison with the flamboyant Lloyd George, the 'Wizard of Wales', was described by one of his friends as 'a small man with the beatific smile of one who has seen the heavens open'.

What I admired about him was his serenity in adversity, and the calm manner in which he refused to be disturbed by gossip, rumour and

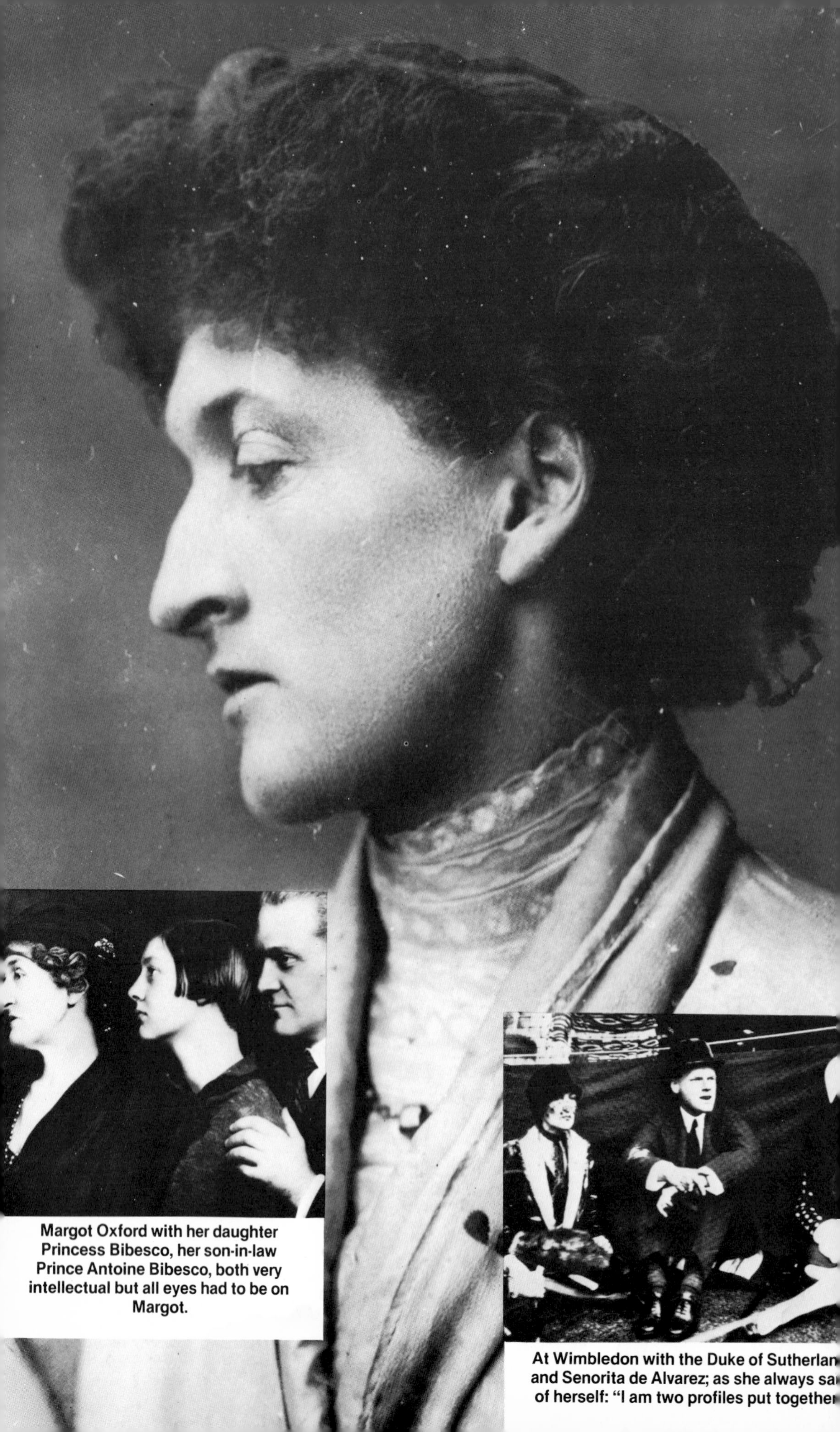

Margot Oxford with her daughter Princess Bibesco, her son-in-law Prince Antoine Bibesco, both very intellectual but all eyes had to be on Margot.

At Wimbledon with the Duke of Sutherlan and Senorita de Alvarez; as she always sa of herself: "I am two profiles put together

personal attack. He continually quoted the aphorism on a mantelpiece at Blenheim Palace:

"They say. What say they? Let them say!"

It is a maxim I have often repeated to myself when unkind and untrue things have been said about me.

Lytton Strachey – the most brilliant literary lion of the period, who emerged upon the social scene after the unexpected success of his book *Eminent Victorians* brought him fame, like Byron, overnight – found Margot Asquith 'faintly civilised', but he decided that like so many society people she was unsympathetic.

He wrote in 1918 of her appearance at the opera:

> Her *mauvais ton* is remarkable. She thinks she's the very tip-top, the *grande dame par excellence* and all the rest of it – and every other moment behaving like a kitchen-maid – giggling, looking round and nudging Elizabeth (her daughter). As for music, of course it's never occurred to her such a thing exists. Yet, as one looks at her small weather-beaten (perhaps one should say life-beaten?) countenance one wonders – there does seem a suggestion of something going on underneath!!

Margot Asquith had an amusing and original way of saying things about people which, of course, were repeated from the moment she said them.

"She told enough white lies to ice a cake."

"He's an imitation rough diamond."

"She's a woman without a roof or rafter in her mouth."

Asked if she believed in ghosts, Margot replied:

"Appearances are in their favour!"

Margot Asquith made life amusing for her friends, even while they lived on a razor's edge of what she would say next. Oswald Mosley remembers that at his first dinner party in her house, when he had just made his maiden speech in the House of Commons, Margot seized his hand with a claw-like grip and said:

"Your speech reminded me in some ways of my old friend Lord Randolph Churchill. But, dear boy, do not share his vices, never live with six women at once, it is so weakening!"

Margot's importance in the political world is yet to be written, but two extracts from *Whitehall Diary*, by Thomas Jones, who was in the Cabinet Secretariat, show her power:

> November 12th, 1922
> This came as a great surprise to Asquith, who has been kept in a false paradise by Mrs. Asquith, despite Reading's attempts to make him understand that his term as Prime Minister was at an end.

October 26th, 1923
Will Lloyd George and Asquith draw closer together, or will Sir John Simon and Margot Asquith block any approach?

Lady Oxford was one of the most remarkable female personalities of the century, but when she was old no one was interested in her. It was very sad. She had been fêted and acclaimed all her life. She had also been extremely controversial and she revelled in it.

She was an inveterate *enfant terrible*. She made the most outrageous remarks like: "What a pity when Christopher Columbus discovered America that he ever mentioned it." She smoked her cigarettes through a foot-long ebony holder and she adored the limelight.

But at the end of the Thirties she was growing old. She was hard up and started an Advice Bureau which was a flop; she tried decorating without much success.

She was extremely thin, but still magnificently upright. She had described her face as 'two profiles put together', and her large nose seemed to have grown even larger.

One met her everywhere but she appeared always to be alone. The young had forgotten she had been the wife of one Prime Minister and loved another; that she had prayed with General Booth, and could dance a *pas seul* in the middle of a ballroom and be thought daring!

Poor, tempestuous, flamboyant Margot – she was no longer remarkable – she died in 1945 at the age of eighty-one.

LADY PLUNKET

To me the spirit of the Twenties was the fascinating, fairy-like, adorable Dorothé Plunket. She was also the most exquisite dancer of the period.

She should have been a professional, for her mother was Fanny Ward, the American actress, who was the first person we ever heard of who had her face lifted.

Dorothé had put up her hair when she was only thirteen so that she could wash dishes in a canteen for troops in the war. Jack Barnato, one of the South African diamond millionaires, proposed to her when she was fourteen, and waited three years to marry her.

When he died she took up flying. She had done forty hours solo, preparatory to taking her pilot's exam, when the aeroplane in which she was going to take her test crashed, killing everyone on board.

Dorothé had wanted to be a nurse, but instead she took to driving her car very fast round Brooklands. More than anything she loved to dance. She married Teddy – the good-looking, delightful, six-foot-tall Lord Plunket – and had three adorable sons, one of whom was a page at my wedding.

Dorothé radiated happiness, kindness and sympathy. She was the first person who showed me that a woman should not only try to amuse and entertain other people, but understand, help and encourage them.

Dorothé always made me feel I was the one person she wanted to see, the one person she wanted to listen to, and she had the same effect on everyone she met. The shyest, dullest, most boring man or woman blossomed when she drew them out and smiled at them. No one ever felt lonely or ignored when Dorothé was there.

She was in looks a living personification of Titania. She always seemed too fragile and too lovely to be true; exquisitely dressed, she floated on tiny feet. She was never unkind, she never repeated gossip, she always produced an extenuating excuse for anyone who was criticised.

"I am sure there must be a good reason," Dorothé would say when people denounced something controversial which a young person had done.

"Let's give them a chance," was one of her favourite maxims.

Yet without gossiping, without being catty, she was so amusing, so entrancing to be with. Everyone loved her, men, women and children,

I've met only two women with an irresistible smile, Dorothé and the Queen Mother.

Dorothé, the Hon. David Herbert and Walter Crisham as the 'Spirit of the Twenties.'

and when she died half London was in tears.

Dorothé was very superstitious. She wouldn't put her left arm into a sleeve first, or her left foot into a shoe.

"If you ever put on a garment inside out," she warned me, "you must jump over it three times before you put it on again."

I'm ashamed to say I always follow this advice; for I can't forget how seriously Dorothé took these things.

Dorothé was a close friend of the gentle, shy Duchess of York (later to be Queen Elizabeth).

Prince George was in love with her and so were a dozen other men, but she was devoted to Teddy – her husband. Patrick, the eldest of her three sons, became Master of the Household to the Queen.

But she had friends in every walk of life.

No one could resist her charm, and when she gave exhibition dances and charity balls in private houses, the audience were clapping her personally as much as they applauded her undoubted talents.

Dorothé and her husband were burnt to death in America when the aeroplane in which they were travelling caught fire.

This was, I felt, a bitter waste; for Dorothé had contributed nothing to flying, only to life and my life in particular.

I have often said just because she said it:

"Let's give them another chance."

As a wife and mother with her clever, always calm and unruffled husband and of course the irrepressible Gresby.

Jean, who strikes strong politicians dumb with terror and fights for what she believes in like an avenging archangel, with her son Gresby.

All at sea, which is something she never is, with that clear, cutting, rapier-like brain.

JEAN ROOK

The Empress of Fleet Street, the most feared woman columnist in the country, she is a star with sharp points and has 'got there' by sheer hard work and a two-edged tongue not like an asp, but a stiletto.

She has a glamour which, mixed with her positive, vital vibrations is somewhat bewildering on first acquaintance. She has an hypnotic magnetism which compels people to bare their souls, when they have no wish to do anything of the sort.

Politicians whom Jean Rook wants to interview have an urgent meeting in the Western Isles, and members of the Jet Set leave for the Sahara.

But I love and admire Jean for several reasons.

First, because she is the one journalist – like the House of Commons Lobby Correspondents of the Thirties – to whom I can tell an explosive secret, say "Don't publish this," and she won't.

Secondly, because she never lies or invents anything to 'make a story'.

Thirdly, because although she is formidable, witty and often 'takes the mickey' out of one, she never throws her victim, like some of her imitators, into a cesspool.

Jean looks under the polished veneer, the hypocrisy, the pretentiousness, and she does find out what makes a person tick.

When I do that to her I find something very different from the Dragon Empress. She is perceptive, intuitive and curious. She has courage, ambition, drive and guts.

She will kill me for saying so, but secretly she is irrepressibly idealistic.

Underneath the tough Fleet Street outer crust there is still a wide-eyed young girl who believes in God and is ready to find life in all its varied aspects an exciting adventure.

She has a charming, quiet, clever husband who is a rock to her raging sea.

She has a small, very intelligent son, Gresby, whom they both adore.

She has a home, ex-directory, whose address is kept hidden even from her friends.

Both she and Gresby finish their letters to those they love with XXX.

Sir Philip, the Prince of Wales and Winston Churchill. Ambitious, Sir Philip would 'lobby' friends to 'put in a word' for him.

One of the most exciting, tantalising personalities of the time, Sir Philip was a brilliant polo player and his team No. 1.

SIR PHILIP SASSOON

Dark, sleek, handsome, enigmatic, immensely rich, Sir Philip Sassoon was the grandson of a Rothschild, a dedicated lover of the Arts, and one of the most exciting, tantalising personalities of the era.

I met him in his London home in Park Lane in a room which had just been fantastically decorated in black and sepia by the Spanish painter, Sert.

"It is very beautiful," I said.

"A background for beautiful women like you!" he replied.

As he spoke I knew there was something wrong. His lips flattered – he was noted for his flattery – but his eyes were hard and impenetrable – empty of any emotion.

He interested me, and the pink flamingos at Trent Park, his house in Hertfordshire, were a strange exotic sight. Guests were called with every morning paper published, there were buttonholes for the men and corsages for the women taken to their bedrooms before dinner.

At Lympne there was astonishing Babylonian luxury with terraces and flowery gardens, jade green pools and swimming baths, rooms in silver, blue, orange and lapis.

It was as Chips Channon wrote – "a strange hydro for this strangest of sinister men".

And he added:

"Though Jewish he hated Jews. What he really loved were jewelled elephants and contrasting colours – the bizarre and the beautiful!"

He was a wonderful provider. When Winston Churchill was asked why Sir Philip had got one of his many Parliamentary appointments, he answered:

"When you are leaving on a long journey for an unknown destination, it is a good plan to attach a restaurant car at the end of the train."

Sir Philip started the war as secretary to General Rawlinson, then had himself transferred as secretary to the Commander-in-Chief. He was supposed to have wired a florist:

"Stop flowers to Lady Rawlinson, but send them to Lady Haig."

Later when Lloyd George became Prime Minister he wired:

"Send flowers to Mrs. Lloyd George."

On Easter Sunday a woman friend telegraphed Sir Philip:

"Christ is risen, apply for secretaryship!"

Sir Philip was everything that was cultured, sohpisticated, civilised. His knowledge of Art was unsurpassed. But – there was something wrong!

When Ronald stayed at Trent he found Sir Philip a strange, lonely, unreal, un-English figure, flitting through the vast rooms filled with amazing examples of Art, yet somehow aloof from the ordinary passions, difficulties and necessities of life.

I learnt that when Sir Philip was very young he had loved a girl who refused to marry him and then died.

It captured my imagination and I wrote a novel with a plot which centred round reincarnation. It was called *The Black Panther*, Sir Philip was the hero – his houses in Park Lane, Trent and the House of Commons were the background.

But Harold Nicolson had a different explanation for those hard eyes, the aura of loneliness, the unreality, and wrote:

> People who care overmuch for the works of man end by losing all sense of the works of God, and even their friends become for them, mere pieces of decoration to be put about the room.

GORDON SELFRIDGE

It is a standard American success story, except that the boy born in Ripon, Wisconsin became the greatest and most spectacular shopkeeper in England.

Gordon Selfridge had an ambitious mother of Scottish descent who fired his imagination, and he made remarks like:

"Profits are not the only prize," and "It is elevating to work, and superb to accomplish."

Through sheer hard work he became staff director of the Marshall Field organisation and came to England in 1906.

"What an advantage, beginning life all over again, and in London!" he cried.

Selfridges in Oxford Street opened in a snow blizzard on 15 March 1909 – flags of twenty nations, an army trumpeter, flowers, 'every gas bracket trimmed with simlax', a First-Aid room, lifts and an aerial garden were all sensational to London shoppers.

Selfridges advertising was "London's lowest prices always," the net profit in 1919 was £372,000 and he announced a profit-sharing scheme for the staff.

The following year Gordon Selfridge at sixty-four was at his peak physically and mentally. In a review they sang:

Mr. Asquith is now an Earl,
Oxford is his seat,
But Mr. Selfridge still remains
The Earl of Oxford Street.

His daughter, who was charming, married Prince Wiasemsky and Gordon moved in new social circles. He played poker with Sir Thomas Lipton and Sir Ernest Cassell, he bought a 900-ton steam yacht *Conqueror*, and started his Election-night parties in 1923. Everyone who was anyone was invited.

The 'Bright Young People' gate-crashed his parties and his store. One 'game' was 'Follow-my-Leader' through Selfridges.

Then Gordon expanded into another world – he became 'friends' with the glamorous, exotic toast of two capitals, Gaby Delys and then with Jenny Dolly. She and her sister Rosie were Hungarian cabaret dancers.

The Lancashire Cotton Queen cutting a length of Lancashire cotton at Selfridges. Gordon always had new ideas!

The Dolly Sisters fascinated many men — mostly millionaires.

The "Dollies and their collies" were sensational publicity and their clothes also kept them in the public eye.

Gaby liked diamonds, she and Gordon would go into the store when it was closed and she would help herself to anything she fancied. Jenny Dolly preferred Cartier.

She had emerald bracelets which reached to her elbow, a necklace of the same stones and a solitaire ring the size of an ice-cube.

Gordon was in love with her for twenty-four years and spent two million pounds between 1924 and 1931, the bulk of it on Jenny.

He bought an interest in Le Touquet Casino. Jenny and Rosie had unlimited credit there and at Deauville. One night at Deauville Jenny won £40,000 then lost it and £40,000 more.

Jenny eventually lost all her money and later committed suicide. Gordon, having had nearly £100,000 a year, died at eighty-three leaving personal belongings worth less than £2,000.

When I first met Gordon Selfridge he was a dynamo of energy, activity and ideas. Then in the middle Twenties, like many other old men, he wanted to rediscover his youth.

He was lonely. His mother was dead and so was his wife. His virile temperament revolted in a state of panic from the inevitable – old age and death.

He would be seen 'out on the Town' until three in the morning, and be at his desk in the store at nine o'clock.

"I don't want to rest," he protested when he was nearly eighty. "I want to go on – and on – and on."

He had a fanatical faith in his star, an unextinguishable belief in his destiny.

The President with his attractive French wife. My novel on Senegal is called *Women Have Hearts*.

The President has the most charming good manners.

The President in Paris with General Charles de Gaulle.

HIS EXCELLENCY
PRESIDENT LÉOPOLD SÉDAR SENGHOR

When I studied the history of Symbolism for a novel I was writing with a background of the Belle Epoque, I never expected actually to meet a Symbolist poet.

The name of my book, *The Flame is Love*, was taken from Verlaine's poem 'L'amour toujours monte comme la flamme'. It has now been filmed.

Symbolism, which means freedom of the imagination and unfettered self-expression, has done for poetry what Impressionism – representing a revolt against current standards and conventions – did for painting.

The most modern and greatest Symbolist French poet of today is President Léopold Sédar Senghor of Senegal.

His poems express vividly Negritude which has been his passionate crusade since he was a young man.

Negritude is the music, the dancing, the sculpture and spirit of the black races. The President invented the idea of it and in 1930 dedicated himself to raising the status of the Negroes, giving them faith in themselves and rousing in the world an appreciation of black culture.

President Senghor's books passionately demonstrate his ideas – *Négritude et Humanisme* – being number one of three large volumes entitled *Liberté*.

He has also written other books, and of course his outstanding and moving poems which express his own inner vision and desires.

'Honour' and 'noble' are two of the words which mean much to him.

1. *Un bouclier d'honneur ne les quittait jamais ni la lance royale . . .*
2. *Me voici rendu à mon peuple et à mon honneur . . .*
3. *Noble devait être ta race et bien née la femme de Timbo qui te berçait le soir au rythme nocturne de la terre . . .*

One of his loveliest **Chantes d'Ombre* is *Femme Noire*, the last verse being:

4. *Femme nue, femme noire,*
   Je chante ta beauté qui passe, forme que je fixe dans l'Éternel.
   Avant que le Destin jaloux ne te réduise en cendres pour nourrir les racines de la vie.

But the President is not only a poet. When Lord Mountbatten asked him to receive me in Dakar in 1979 I was taken by the British Ambassador to his huge white palace overlooking the beautiful bay.

When I shook hands with President Senghor he had that aura of power that I seek for in all outstanding celebrities, but he also had a sensitivity which shone through him like a light.

In 1937, when he was thirty-one, Léopold Senghor was a Professeur de Lettres et Grammaire au Lycée Descartes à Tours. Three years later he was a prisoner of war in la Charité-sur-Loire, but after twelve months was released through illness. He was in the Resistance and when the war ended he became Député de Sénégal à l'Assemblée Constituante.

In 1960 he became the 1st President of the Republic of Senegal, three years later Honorary Doctor of the Université of Paris, and the following year he won the *Grand Prix Industriel de Poésie.*

Awards, honours, recognition from many Universities have followed year by year.

The President has a beautiful French wife and a son Phillippe, and he told me his great wish is for his son to be truly bilingual. He believes it is most important now the world has grown so much easier to encompass, that we should all speak each other's languages.

We spoke of the United World Colleges of which Lord Mountbatten was the Patron and which he believed are a practical effort towards world peace. Students of every nation, colour and creed work together and get to know and understand each other. There are five students from Senegal at the Atlantic College at St. Donat's in Wales.

"I would like," President Senghor said, "to have a United World College in Dakar and the President, the Prince of Wales, to visit Senegal."

I am sure he will get his wish, for His Excellency is a man who, all his life, has used his power to further what he believes to be right for his people.

★*J'ai touché seulement la chaleur de votre main brune,*
je me suis nommé: Afrika!

1. A breast-plate of honour never leaves me nor the royal lance.
2. Here I am given over to my people and to my honour.
3. Your race should be noble and well-born the wife of Timbo who puts you in your cradle in the evening to the nocturnal rhythm of the earth.

★ *Songs of the Shadow* is *Black Woman.*

4. Naked woman, black woman.
   I sing of your passing beauty, a shape I set in the Eternal.
   Before jealous Destiny reduces you to ashes to nourish the roots of life.

★ I have only touched the warmth of your brown hand, I am called: Africa!

ERNEST SIMPSON

Good-looking with a very square chin, he gave the impression his collar was too tight. He held himself stiffly as one might have expected from an Officer in the Coldstream Guards, and was so English in everything he said and did that it was difficult to remember he was half American.

In 1919 all I wanted was to dance. To please me, after my father was killed in 1918, my mother rented a small house in London, but she knew very few people having always lived in Worcestershire.

Among a mere handful of friends and acquaintances were Major and Mrs. Kerr-Smiley who had a large house in Belgrave Square.

Mrs. Kerr-Smiley was an American, small, attractive, kind and hospitable. Every Sunday she gave a *thé dansant*. I was thrilled to receive an invitation.

At first my mother was horrified at the idea. She had always been very religious, and playing cards and dancing were two things we had never been allowed to do on a Sunday.

"But I must go," I pleaded with her. "All my friends are going. How can I refuse?"

"Very well," my mother said. "You can go, but you must teach in a Sunday School to make up for it."

I accepted this compromise with delight and hurried off every Sunday morning to the children's Sunday School, St. Paul's, Knightsbridge.

Feeling I had paid for breaking the Sabbath I would in the afternoon arrive eagerly at the *thé dansant*.

Among the young men I met at Mrs. Kerr-Smiley's was her brother Ernest. He was a good dancer, clever but shy.

Although in consequence some of the other girls found him difficult to talk to, I always had so much to say that no one was shy with me for long.

I think Ernest rather liked me, but his sister often said warningly:

"It's no use you girls losing your hearts to Ernest – he has to marry money!"

Once when my mother was away I wrote to her:

> As usual I enjoyed being at Maud Kerr-Smiley's on Sunday. Ernest took me home in a taxi and tried to kiss me. Such cheek! Of course I didn't let him!

Three of his four wives.

Mary.

Wallis.

Averil.

Ten years later Ernest married for the second time, and his sister asked me to the first luncheon party she gave for his wife who had also been married before – her name was Wallis Warfield.

When I was introduced to her I was frankly disappointed. Ernest had always been smart. His sister Maud had always been exquisitely dressed and although she was not pretty she was extremely elegant.

Wallis wore a dowdy black dress and a shapeless hat which accentuated her very bad complexion. She had large hands and used them too much. She was however very vivacious but obviously determined to be somewhat aggressively American.

She had brought with her to show the party half a dozen handkerchiefs on which were printed some rather bawdy parodies of nursery rhymes. The other women laughed but I thought them in rather bad taste, and they were not my type of humour.

Gradually in the next few years I began to see and hear a lot about the Simpsons, and although they were not often seen at the famous Embassy Club on a Thursday night, or at other night clubs, I seldom went to a theatre without finding them in the stalls.

Wallis became smarter, she had her complexion improved miraculously by a new method of face massage given her by a Canadian. She also became much more charming and developed a natural gaiety which made everything she said sound witty.

I heard from other friends how well Ernest was doing in his father's business of ship-broking and how clever many men found him.

Thelma Furness, who had supplanted Freda Dudley Ward in the Prince of Wales's affections, 'took up' the Simpsons. Wallis became her greatest friend, so they moved into the Prince's circle.

Thelma was a charming person whom I loved. She was beautiful, intelligent and very kind. Everyone thought she gave the Prince a happiness he had never known before. She was discreet about her position, and the most critical of Court officials admitted that she was 'no trouble'.

In 1934 I and a friend met Thelma in the street. She was looking very lovely and elegant.

"I'm off to America," she told us.

"The Prince won't like that," my friend replied. "What will he do without you?"

Thelma smiled.

"I've asked Wallis to look after him. He will be safe with her."

We walked on.

"Wallis may not be beautiful," I said reflectively, "but I think nowadays she has become very fascinating."

When Thelma belatedly returned from America, it was learnt that her *affaire* with the Prince was at an end.

Wallis blossomed, her furs, her clothes from Schiaparelli, her sets of fantastic jewels, sapphires, rubies, emeralds and Queen Alexandra's earrings set in a pair of diamond clips left no one in any doubt that whisperings which were growing and growing about her and the Prince of Wales were true.

Ernest having at first been there, though in the background, now faded. He was away on business in America or on the Continent. Wallis went with the Prince and a party to France, Austria, Cannes and a cruise in the Adriatic.

The sneers and sniggers about the absent husband would have hurt any man, let alone one as reserved and introverted as Ernest. The Prince's close friends coined the phrase the 'unImportance of being Ernest', and jokes about husbands who were 'cuckolded' flooded from the Clubs and the Stock Exchange.

In January, 1936, King George V died – the Prince of Wales was now King.

Almost immediately I heard that Ernest had gone to America and Wallis intended to divorce him. No one knew whether he had a real attachment for someone else as was stated in the petition or if he was behaving in the time-honoured manner of a gentleman in providing the required evidence.

He gave no interviews to the Press. If he discussed what had happened with anyone it was not repeated to me or anyone I knew.

Wallis's divorce petition was put down for hearing at the Ipswich Assizes and the American Press was full of predictions that she would marry the King! When finally the ban was lifted from the English newspapers, Simpson became the most notorious name from one end of the world to the other.

There is no need to write of what happened after that, it has been recorded a thousand times in documents, books and on television.

I did not see or hear of Ernest until after the war when I learnt he had married for a third time, been widowed and had now married a very old friend of mine, Princess George Imeretinsky.

Averil had taken part in the cabarets and pageants I had introduced at the end of the Twenties and beginning of the Thirties to raise money for charity.

She had been 'Green' in the Superstitious Ball, 'The Golden Arrow' at the Train Ball, and had won the first women's car race that took place at Brooklands which I organised in 1931.

She was very attractive and a talented person with a sweet, loving nature whose marriage when she was very young to a Georgian Prince had been a disaster.

She had also suffered from explosive publicity of the shaming kind, through no fault of her own. Her father, the wealthy Sir John Mullens, had an elder daughter, Elvira Barney, who had been charged in 1932 with murder.

At the time it was a *cause célèbre* with the newspapers publishing every unpleasant detail.

Spoilt and wilful Mrs. Elvira Barney after an unhappy marriage had drifted into a life of flagrant immorality. She drank and lived openly with a worthless young man who existed solely on her money.

Her story at the trial was that one night they quarrelled and when she learnt he was proposing to leave her, she threatened to shoot herself. In the struggle to prevent her doing so the revolver went off and killed him.

Unfortunately there were witnesses to swear they had heard Mrs. Barney say: "I will shoot you," and later to scream: "Laugh baby! Laugh for the last time!"

She was saved dramatically from being hanged by the brilliance of her defending counsel, Sir Patrick Hastings, the greatest advocate at the Bar. Only Sir Patrick could have got her off!

He told me how she never thanked him, and he only saw her once more. He was driving his car up a steep hill from Boulogne on the Paris road when a long, low car dashed round the corner on the wrong side, nearly killing him and his chauffeur, who was sitting beside him.

"Did you see who was driving that car, Sir?" he asked. "It was Mrs. Barney."

From such a relative and from the publicity which naturally hurt and shocked her, Averil found sanctuary with Ernest.

I dined with them at their house in Phillimore Gardens. The big, high rooms were beautifully decorated with the books Ernest loved to read and the fine pictures and furniture he had painstakingly collected over the years.

We were just four, Averil and Ernest, my husband and I. The conversation was intelligent, stimulating without there being any need for gossip or uncomfortable reminiscences of the past.

Looking at Ernest sitting at the top of the table, his shoulders straight, his chin very square, and listening to his quiet, calm voice I was aware how much he had altered. There was a new power and determination about him, a strength he had never had before.

He was a man who had passed through deep waters, and who had done battle not with the world but with himself. He had won and was the Captain of his soul. I could feel this force emanating from him, and I know that Averil, listening to him with adoring eyes, could feel it too.

Only when we left and Ernest saw us to the front door and I kissed him goodbye, did I say:

"I am so very glad you are happy Ernest, no one deserves it more, no one could have behaved better in the Hell you passed through."

His fingers tightened on mine until they hurt as he said very quietly:

"Thank you, Barbara, I suppose in time one will forget."

Eleanor loved flamenco music, the bull ring, Nomad gypsies, Andalusian plains, cafes, the circus, baby elephants and horses.

Eleanor adored her father, "a natural spell-binder — dazzling and confident."

Eleanor with 'Togare' the wild tiger tamer. She loved tigers, animal and human.

LADY ELEANOR SMITH

It was to be expected that Lord Birkenhead's daughter would be a personality and Eleanor was certainly that and a great deal more.

She was dark, like her father the famous F.E. Smith, first Lord Birkenhead, with wild hair swept back from her oval forehead. She had black eyes which could flash with anger or excitement and there was an air of purpose and urgency about her, as if she had to hurry to get everything she could out of life.

Eleanor told us she was of gypsy descent.

"My great-grandmother's name was Bathsheba," she said. "She was dark, handsome and temperamental, with brilliant eyes, an olive complexion and jew-black ringlets."

Eleanor made it sound so convincing that we believed every word of it, and accepted that her great interest in gypsies and circus people was due to the fact that she was a blood sister of theirs, and therefore drawn to them instinctively.

It was not until many years later that her brother, Freddie Birkenhead, was to expose the truth. He explained that their grandmother, a nonconformist schoolmistress, had a dark complexion. He wrote:

> This was my sister's sole and slender excuse for claiming a gypsy descent. Her hallucination about Bathsheba led to some serious misunderstandings. Not only did I foolishly accept her account and quote it in a previous book, but I also misled Sir Winston Churchill into introducing this travesty of fact in his brilliant work *Great Contemporaries*. Later it reached Nazi Germany at the end of the war that our family had been booked for total extermination on account of its impure gypsy blood.

Eleanor wrote 'Women's Gossip' for an evening newspaper and became a film critic.

She hated both jobs and threw them up at a moment's notice to wander with the great Carno Circus. She was completely under the spell of the Big Top, and even on one occasion took the place of a bare-back rider who was ill.

She wrote several delightful novels: *Red Wagon* was the first, which was a great success, then *Ballerina* – inspired by Anna Pavlova before she died – was adapted for the stage, with Frances Doble (Sacheverell

Sitwell's sister-in-law) and Anton Dolin as the stars.

It was put on at the Scala Theatre, and during the dress rehearsal a strange thing happened. The stage revolved to show a woodland glade, and a snow-white figure in a fluffy *tutu*, its head bound with swans' feathers, moved on to the stage.

Eleanor, watching from the stalls, thought that Frances seemed much smaller, then as the figure glided into the spotlight she saw that it was Anna Pavlova!

Anton Dolin saw it too. He gripped Eleanor's hand and went deadly pale.

"This is uncanny," he muttered, "it's awful . . . what have we done? Oh God – why did we ever bring up the past?"

Dolin had put on his understudy Borek, and now the white form stood effortlessly upon one *pointe*, pirouetted three times – something Frances couldn't do – and drifted like swansdown into Borek's arms as the curtain fell.

Three other people who had also watched were white and dazed.

"We can't all have seen – what we saw," one of them mumbled.

Afraid, Dolin and Eleanor ran to the pass door, Frances stood there on the stage.

"I'm sorry . . ." she said to Dolin, "let's take it again."

"Take it again. Why?"

"I couldn't dance. I must be awfully tired. My mind suddenly seemed to go blank. Will someone get me a glass of water?"

Later Dolin affirmed:

"We can't deny it. For a moment that particular spirit from the past took possession of Frances's mind and body."

On the last night Frances Doble untied her pink ballet shoes and declared:

"I shall never walk upon a stage again, as long as I live."

She never did.

Eleanor adored her father, but the Birkenheads always teased each other. One day Lord Birkenhead came home with the news that he had been offered a lot of money to write a series of articles called 'Milestones in My Life'. His family asked which incidents he proposed to use. He told them.

"You might have put in your marriage!" Lady Birkenhead said reproachfully.

"And the birth of your first child," Eleanor added.

"I said milestones, my dears," Lord Birkenhead replied, "not millstones."

One of Eleanor's claims to fame was that in 1923 she was charged by the Men and Women's Christian Temperance Union with having 'publicly smoked a cigarette on the quad of Magdalene College'.

Eleanor was one of the organisers of the Bright Young People, but it

Gertrude Lawrence

The Hispania-Suiza, the Stage-Door Johnnies in white tie and tails, the orchids, the adoration, the applause — that is Gertie.

1 C. B. Cochran wrote "our most brilliant actress. There is none so sparkling, more witty or with such a perfection of poise."
Douglas Fairbanks, handsome, captivatingly attractive with an irresistible smile.

2 "A never-failing sense of fun and astonishing touches of exquisite tenderness in the right places."

3 "No other actress has her quality of dramatic radiance."
Ronald Squires a very easy, very civilised gentlemanly actor with a twinkle in his eyes and an engaging sense of humour.

This painting by Sir John Lavery of a Court at Buckingham Palace in 1931 when King George V and Queen Mary received the debutantes is unique.
When I tried to find it no one knew where it was and the Press office at Buckingham Palace assured me it did not exist. Then I discovered it in my own Scrapbook! I was presented twice in the same way. First by my mother, secondly on my marriage.
The Gentlemen at Arms in their plumed helmets, the Diplomatic Corps resplendent in gold braid and decorations, the Peeresses glittering like Christmas trees, and the debutantes with their trains and Prince of Wales' Feathers were a pageant I will never forget.

A Court at Buckingham Palace

Among the celebrities and debutantes in this picture are Sir John Lavery's lovely wife, whose face was on the Irish Bank notes, the resplendent Marchioness of Londonderry, the greatest political hostess of the time, presenting Lady Helen Stewart; the Countess of Oxford in profile; the Viscountess Wimborne with a huge and better diamond tiara than anyone else, Miss Diana Churchill — Winston's elder red-haired daughter — Miss Margaret Whigham, the most beautiful debutante of the year, who later married the Duke of Argyll, Miss Baba Beaton, whose brother Cecil was making a name for himself with his Brownie and Lady Georgina Curzon presented by her mother the exquisite Viscountess Curzon.

A Court at Buckingham Palace

Millicent Duchess of Sutherland

Her son, the 5th Duke of Sutherland

Beautiful, so that she was every man's ideal woman, with a charm that captivated everyone to whom she spoke. It was in a gown like this that the Duchess received her guests on the staircase at Stafford House wearing a crown-shaped tiara.
With it she wore the magnificent necklace of huge diamonds which had belonged to Marie Antoinette. Kings and Crown Princes from Europe climbed the staircase and only when they left did she relax and on one occasion squirted a siphon of soda water on top of the heads of some lingering guests below. Dunrobin Castle in Scotland where the Duchess reigned as Queen is so magical and lovely that I have featured it in many of my novels.

was never one exclusive group.

A young man bet Eleanor she would not sleep the night in the Chamber of Horrors at Madame Tussaud's. She went there at 9.15 p.m. with Zita Yungman, and hid when the officials called 'closing time'.

They endured the creepy atmosphere, the draught which blew through the hall rustling the ropes of the men who had been hanged, for three hours.

By one o'clock they were cramped and cold. Eleanor suggested they should go upstairs, lift the little Princes in the Tower out of their bed and sleep in it.

They were just about to move the little Princes when a night-watchman found them. He was terrified until he realised they were live.

"We're locked in. Please let us out," Eleanor explained.

"My God!" he exclaimed, "you naughty girls! Won't you just catch it!"

Eleanor was often outrageous, but she was always original, adventurous, receptive and above all, full of the joy of living.

The Twenties would not have been such fun without her.

Dorothy live at Drury Lane and at the Palladium – at all times larger than life.

DOROTHY SQUIRES

I had heard vaguely of her turbulent quarrels, her unhappiness when Roger Moore left her, her numerous law-cases and many other things. I knew she had an enormous voice because, like Harry Secombe and Shirley Bassey, she came from Wales.

But nothing prepared me for a very small, pretty person with a little-girl hair-do and exquisite feet.

Dorothy Squires picked me up at the studios of L.B.C. after I had just finished making an Album with the Royal Philharmonic Orchestra and I had the same wonderful famous producer, Norman Newell, as she had.

I asked her to lunch, she came and cried all through my recording *I'll See You Again* because it reminded her of Roger. She insisted, although I tried to refuse, that I should go to her concert.

Every year Dorothy takes a theatre to sing to her fans, she does not advertise but by instinct they all turn up to hear her.

This year she had taken the Palladium on Guy Fawkes night, the 5th of November, which everyone thought was mad.

"The worst night to sell a seat in any theatre!" they told me.

The Palladium was packed from floor to ceiling, there wasn't a square inch to put a mouse! Dorothy took the roof off! Where she keeps that voice I couldn't imagine!

Then she told the audience how she had met me, how much she loved my *Album of Love Songs*, and she made them all sing *If I Was The Only Girl in the World* to me as I sat in the Royal Box.

She followed it with *I'll See You Again* with tears in her eyes and then told everyone to buy my Album.

It was an unbelievable tribute from a professional to an amateur, from one woman to another!

I think only a Celt could have been so generous in thought, word and deed!

On her Christmas card to me she wrote:

> No Queen has and ever will look as beautiful as you did in the Royal Box of the London Palladium.
>
> Love, Dorothy

Her heart is as big as her voice.

She loved dressing up. Here she is in a film. At the 'Jewel Ball' the best jewels had been taken so as Coral and Jade Lois and I wore wigs to match our gowns and were sensational!

The Earl of Pembroke, charming to meet, with a great sense of humour, at the coming-of-age of his eldest son Lord Herbert.

Lois, impulsive, original and very unpredictable. She was a social rebel and snapped her fingers at the older generation which was exceedingly courageous in those days.

THE HON. LOIS STURT

In the Twenties, Lois Sturt, Lady Allington's daughter, was the only one of my close friends who was lucky enough to get into the movies. She had a part in *The Glorious Adventure* as Nell Gwynne. She couldn't have been better cast.

She was in real life, pure 'Restoration'. She had dark flashing eyes, was impetuous, fearless and completely unpredictable. There was nothing she wouldn't do. She loved dressing up and was to be in all the charity pageants I produced.

Lois fell in love with the Earl of Pembroke, older than herself and already notorious for his many love-affairs. He was a peer of great social consequence, with vast estates and a wife who moved in Court circles.

He was completely captivated by Lois and, perhaps for the first time in his life, really in love. They went everywhere together, making no effort to hide their infatuation. Since they were both extremely well known soon the gossip columns hinted at the association. Finally he asked his wife for a divorce.

Dignified, reserved, an aristocrat to her fingertips, the Countess listened to him in silence. She was hurt, humiliated and unhappy. I think her first instinct was to escape from the sordid degradation of clinging to a husband who no longer wanted her and who was parading his 'paramour' for all the world to see.

Then she looked at Wilton, the fantastically beautiful house in which generations of her husband's family had lived; she saw the priceless furniture, the pictures, the famous gardens with their fountains and army of gardeners. She also saw her children coming home to find another woman at the head of the dining table, another woman wearing the family jewels.

She saw all her care of the people on the estate forgotten, her charities neglected, her friends no longer invited. She knew too, that her monthly tea-parties with Queen Mary would no longer be possible – small intimate occasions which meant a lot to her.

"No," she said quietly to her husband, "I will never give you a divorce. This is our children's home and mine. I shall stay here. You must do what you wish."

Furious, he raged and pleaded, but she was adamant. He and Lois took a villa in the South of France together. People found them fun, amusing and carefree, although they both lived too hard and drank too much. His wife continued to have tea with Queen Mary.

Inevitably the riotous life took its toll. Reggie Pembroke was not young enough to stand the pace. He was ill; Lois found other men more amusing. Finally he went back to Wilton. His wife accepted him without reproach. The great house, the estates were his and he knew in his heart it was where he belonged.

"How wise you were, dear, not to give Reggie a divorce," an intimate friend said sometime later.

"Divorce is no cure for unhappiness," was the reply.

Lois always had rather unusual men in love with her and finally she married Viscount Tredegar, who was a character straight out of fiction.

He had lived in the Vatican as Privy Chamberlain of the Sword and Cape to the Pope, he stood for Parliament as a Conservative candidate for Limehouse, and made himself an expert on unemployment and housing because he owned most of Bow and Bromley.

He was the world's leading authority on John Donne: he was a gourmet; a music-lover; a poet; the owner of a menagerie and had remarkable gifts as a bird-tamer.

Evan Tredegar, who looked like a Prince of the Renaissance, wore huge rings and dressed in picturesque flowing capes and coloured waistcoats. His castle in Wales, Tredegar Park, was full of treasures. The one he liked best of them all was his macaw who pecked everyone.

In the house in South Street, where he and Lois lived when they were in London, there was a cage of live monkeys halfway up the stairs.

Lois had a bathroom in which, while lying in the bath she could turn on a light and see silhouetted on the ceiling all the exotic Roman pictures which had decorated the brothels in Pompeii.

Evan Tredegar's mother as a hobby made exquisite copies of birds' nests. There was a rumour that she had also made a large model with mud, so that she could sit in it herself.

Lois laughed and drank, and drank and laughed until she died. She was a personality, a Rabelaisian character who was born too late.

MILLICENT, DUCHESS OF SUTHERLAND

She was old when I first met her, but she was still one of the most beautiful women I have ever seen in my life.

The glory of the Edwardian era has been summed up in the words of Vita Sackville West in *The Edwardians*:

> Deevy parties at Stafford House always. And Millie looking like a Goddess, with a golden train halfway down the stairs. The charm of that woman! Everybody will be there.

An artist fainted at the Duchess's beauty when he saw her at a fancy-dress ball. During the war she had her own hospital at Calais. She wore a special white uniform with a huge ruby cross on her breast. My husband was taken there desperately wounded, and he told me:

"She was so beautiful, she made dying men, like myself, want to live."

Tall, with a curved feminine figure, she had perfect bone construction, huge expressive eyes, golden hair, a fabulous white skin, and a smile which made your heart turn over in your breast, it was so entrancing.

Duchess Millicent; the Sutherlands always call their Duchesses by their Christian names to distinguish them; was naturally breathtakingly beautiful, but she also took 'trouble' with herself.

When she was over eighty she always made up her eyelashes, rouged and powdered her face, and arranged her well-waved hair before she allowed anyone to see her.

In the Twenties I came to know the exquisite Duchess very well and I loved her. She used to talk to me of her success as a beauty; of her parties, balls and receptions; of the incredible grandeur and luxury of her life, married to a man who was treated as the King of Scotland.

Later, when she was widowed and had married again unhappily, the Duchess wrote a book about her life called *That Fool of a Woman*. But her son disapproved, so he bought up every copy and destroyed them.

"I always loved stupid men," she confided in me, "it was such a relief to get away from the clever ones, to relax and take off my kid gloves."

The Duke of Sutherland, with 1,250,000 acres, was the largest landowner in the British Isles. He had his own private train and railway line

Millicent with her daughter Rosemary, later the Countess of Dudley.

Stafford House, 1901.

and owned a coal-mine. A navvy seeing him set off from Dunrobin, his castle in Sutherland, said:

"There, that's what I call a real dook – there 'e is a-driving 'is own engine, on 'is own train, and a-burning 'is own bloody coals."

The Duchess told me how she had met her husband.

"It was just chance! How much that counts in all our lives! The Duke came to stay with my father and mother and of course, as I was only sixteen and still in the schoolroom, it was most unlikely I should ever set eyes on him. But at the last moment it was discovered there would be thirteen at dinner. I was hurriedly dressed in my best frock and sent downstairs."

"And the Duke fell in love with you?"

"As soon as he saw me! He proposed shortly afterwards, to the consternation of my parents! But we were married on my seventeenth birthday."

The Duke of Sutherland was one of the first really rich men to sense that the social revolution would slowly undermine his wealth. He could still pin a £1,000 note on his wife's pillow while she slept, but he started to dispose of some of his property and Stafford House in 1912 was the first to go.

It was of Stafford House where Queen Victoria said to Duchess Harriet, "I come from my home to your palace."

But nothing could be more lovely or more like a fairy palace than Dunrobin Castle, the ancestral home of the Sutherland family in Scotland, with its turrets and towers silhouetted against the purple moss.

It was here that King Edward VII stayed after the serious operation for appendicitis which postponed his Coronation.

He and Queen Alexandra arrived in the bay in *The Victoria and Albert* and the King was well enough to drive and autograph the Duke's private railway engine. He also decided to have it copied for the Royal Train.

But with all the glory, the glamour, the luxurious exotic life of the period there was also worry and often deep unhappiness.

Duchess Millicent's eldest son, the 5th Duke, was extremely handsome, tall, fair, blue-eyed like a Viking. When I met him in the Twenties when he was thirty-five, I could not believe any man could be more attractive.

Duchess Millicent told me how when he was very young he had fallen madly in love with the most beautiful woman of the post-war period.

Born in the obscurity of a poor country vicarage, her amazing beauty, what Michael Arlen called 'the golden white beauty of the world's last aristocracy', was so overwhelming that at eighteen she was hastily pushed into marriage with a distinguished and titled cousin.

The were both very unhappy but the most eligible Duke in the whole of Debrett, much younger than she, loved her to distraction. She flirted prettily with him, but her heart was untouched.

At last Duchess Millicent intervened.

"You can have what love affairs you please," she said to her son, "but you must get married. In your position in life it is your duty to produce an heir. Find yourself a wife."

"If I can't have the woman I love," the Duke replied, "I don't care whom I marry. You choose one for me, I'm not interested."

His mother asked three girls to stay. They were all blue-blooded, well mannered, well behaved and pretty enough to carry the family tiaras. The Duke chose the first one he saw.

"She'll do!" he said, and after they had met twice he proposed.

It was a magnificent wedding attended by most of the Royal Family, but after they were married, the much desired heir didn't appear.

It was then that it was discoverd that out of all the girls the Duke might have married, the one he had chosen was barren!

"How could I have known? How could I guess?" Duchess Millicent asked me, and there were tears in her beautiful eyes.

THE HON. DAPHNE VIVIAN
THE MARCHIONESS OF BATH

The most exciting romance of the Twenties was between Viscount Weymouth, heir to the Marquis of Bath, and the lovely vivacious Daphne Vivian.

Daphne was of the new order, a young woman who possessed both brains and beauty. She was tall and slender and she made every other girl in the room seem gawky. Her face would light up and one would find oneself staring speechless at her beauty.

While Daphne inevitably was thought to typify all that was casual and indifferent in the Bright Young People, she was incurably romantic.

She fell in love with Henry and he with her. Henry would have been handsome in any case, but he had broken his nose. This gave him a fascinating raffishness which today still enthralls those who visit Longleat to see the lions, or who watch him on television.

He has worn best of all the elegant young men of the dancing years. He is still a Michael Arlen hero.

Daphne's and Henry's parents decided that it would not be a suitable marriage, they were both too young, too wild and too irresponsible. Henry was told to go round the world and forget Daphne. She was commanded to turn her attentions elsewhere.

This paternal tyranny incited them to immediate rebellion. A month before Henry was due to leave England they made their plans. They took out an ordinary marriage licence and the banns were read three Sundays running, at St. Paul's Knightsbridge.

Henry gave his name as Frederick Thynne, which was of course, his family name, and Daphne used her second name, Winifred. The Press must have been blind, deaf and dumb!

They were married with two Church charladies as witnesses and went to Winchester for the weekend.

Daphne wore her wedding-ring on a chain round her neck and Henry went to America. When he returned all opposition to their wedding was surprisingly removed. Conscience-stricken they felt it would be unkind to tell their families how they had been hoodwinked. So they said nothing.

They were engaged for five months during which time Daphne suffered agonies thinking someone would denounce them.

The were married for the second time at St. Martin-in-the-Fields. I suggested to Daphne she should have her wedding-dress designed by a

Daphne and Henry, who were the most attractive couple in the Twenties. She now writes books with her second husband. He shows the public the lions and treasures of Longleat.

new young designer called Norman Hartnell. It was of white net with gold and silver *fleurs-de-lis*, and she was followed by bridesmaids and pages.

In her autobiography which she wrote as brilliantly as her other books, under the name of Daphne Fielding, she says:

"I felt convinced that the service would be interrupted by an accusing voice, crying out that we were already married."

But nothing happened and they were very, very happy for a great number of years.

Not for ever – there had to be a twist somewhere.

One thing I know, life can never die,
Translucent, splendid, flaming like the sun.
Only our bodies wither and deny
The life force when our strength is done.

We all transmit this wonderful fire
Its force and power from God above
And know eternally it is His
In every act of love.

B.C.

Photographic Credits

Colour

Josephine Baker: Private Collection; Noel Coward: Camera Press, The Garrick Club; Indira Gandhi: Camera Press; Elinor Glyn: The Royal Geographical Society; The Countess Mountbatten of Burma: Broadlands Estate; The Duchess of Sutherland: The Pilgrim Press Limited, Sotheby Parke Bernet and Co.

Black & White

Associated Newspapers Limited: 14 (bottom left); BBC Hulton Picture Library: 22 (top right), 44 (bottom left, right), 76 (bottom right); Cecil Beaton Estate: 122 (top right); Beaverbrook Estate: 28, 70 (top right, bottom); Ben Visuals: 86 (right), 148 (right); Noel Coward Estate: 38 (right), 66 (middle left, bottom right); Fox Photos: 74 (bottom), 134 (top centre); David Higham Associates: 66 (bottom right); The Illustrated London News Picture Library: 160, 188 (top, bottom right); Kobal Collection: 14 (top), 26 (top right), 84 (top right); Lenare: 26 (bottom left); London Express: 92 (bottom right), 104 (top right), 146, 158; National Archives: 98 (top); National Portrait Gallery: 18 (top), 22 (bottom), 34 (bottom right); The National Trust: 102 (top, bottom); New York Public Library: 76 (top left); Popperfoto: 12 (bottom), 14 (bottom right), 40, 44 (top left), 52 (top, bottom right), 72, 80, 104 (bottom right), 114 (top left, middle, bottom), 120 (top left), 122 (left, middle right), 128 (left, bottom right), 134 (bottom), 138 (top, bottom left), 148 (top), 152 (top), 164 (top left), 166 (bottom right), 170 (top left, right); Rainbird Publishing Limited: 122 (bottom right); Rex Features: 86 (left, middle), 92 (bottom left), 166 (top, bottom left); J. Stanley Ltd: 108 (top); Universal Pictorial Press: 178 (top right).